D0077198

Paraeducators in Physical Education

A Training Guide to Roles and Responsibilities

LAUREN J. LIEBERMAN, EDITOR

and

AAPAR

HUMAN KINETICS

Library of Congress Cataloging-in-Publication Data

Paraeducators in physical education : a training guide to roles and responsibilities / Lauren J. Lieberman, editor, and AAPAR.
   p. cm.
  Includes bibliographical references.
  ISBN-13: 978-0-7360-6804-8 (soft cover)
  ISBN-10: 0-7360-6804-X (soft cover)
 1. Physical education teachers--Training of--United States. 2. Teachers' assistants--Training of--United States. 3. Students with disabilities--Education--United States. I. Lieberman, Lauren J., 1965- II. AAPAR (Association)

  GV363.P37 2007
  613.7'11--dc22

                    2007010552

ISBN-10: 0-7360-6804-X
ISBN-13: 978-0-7360-6804-8

Copyright © 2007 by AAPAR

All rights reserved. Except for use in a review, the reproduction or utilization of this work in any form or by any electronic, mechanical, or other means, now known or hereafter invented, including xerography, photocopying, and recording, and in any information storage and retrieval system, is forbidden without the written permission of the publisher.

The Web addresses cited in this text were current as of February 2007, unless otherwise noted.

Acquisitions Editor: Bonnie Pettifor Vreeman; **Managing Editor:** Kathleen Bernard; **Assistant Editor:** Jillian Evans; **Copyeditor:** Alisha Jeddeloh; **Proofreader:** Erin Cler; **Permission Manager:** Dalene Reeder; **Graphic Designer:** Bob Reuther; **Graphic Artist:** Denise Lowry; **Cover Designer:** Keith Blomberg; **Photographer (front cover):** © Human Kinetics; **Photographer (interior):** © Human Kinetics, except where otherwise noted; Sherry Folsom-Meek (pp. 50, 53); Monica Lepore (pp. 4, 6, 8); Scott Modell (pp. 26, 27); Carla Rodriguez (pp. 21, 32, 38, 39, 54, 57, 65); Shawn Stevens (p. 37); **Photo Asset Manager:** Laura Fitch; **Visual Production Assistant:** Joyce Brumfield; **Photo Office Assistant:** Jason Allen; **Printer:** Versa Press

Printed in the United States of America   10 9 8 7 6 5 4 3 2 1

Human Kinetics
Web site: www.HumanKinetics.com

United States: Human Kinetics, P.O. Box 5076, Champaign, IL 61825-5076
800-747-4457
e-mail: humank@hkusa.com

Canada: Human Kinetics, 475 Devonshire Road Unit 100, Windsor, ON N8Y 2L5
800-465-7301 (in Canada only)
e-mail: orders@hkcanada.com

Europe: Human Kinetics, 107 Bradford Road, Stanningley, Leeds LS28 6AT, United Kingdom
+44 (0) 113 255 5665
e-mail: hk@hkeurope.com

Australia: Human Kinetics, 57A Price Avenue, Lower Mitcham, South Australia 5062
08 8372 0999
e-mail: liaw@hkaustralia.com

New Zealand: Human Kinetics, Division of Sports Distributors NZ Ltd., P.O. Box 300 226 Albany, North Shore City, Auckland
0064 9 448 1207
e-mail: info@humankinetics.co.nz

Contents

Preface

It is common practice to include students with disabilities in the general physical education class. Meeting the goals and objectives of everyone in the class can be an overwhelming responsibility for the general physical educator and for the adapted physical educator. Paraeducators are a natural source of support for the physical educators, yet currently there are no requirements or guidelines for paraeducators in physical education. Research has shown that only 43% of children with disabilities who have a paraeducator for support in academic classes also have the paraeducator in physical education (Maurer, 2004). Of the 43% of paraeducators who go to physical education with their student, none have been trained in this area (Maurer, 2004). Aschemeier (2004) reported that only 16% of paraeducators have been trained in physical education.

Therefore, many children with disabilities who need support in academic classes have little or no support in physical education. Several of these paraeducators do not know if physical education attendance is in their contract, on the student's IEP, or required by the district. To make matters worse, there is no designated person at the national, state, or local level to train paraeducators in physical education.

The No Child Left Behind Act has been implemented to ensure that more highly trained teachers and professionals are working with all children. This book is an attempt at improving the knowledge, expertise, and experience of paraeducators so that they can best support students with a disability in physical education.

The topics for this book were gathered from inquiries to general physical educators, adapted physical educators, paraeducators, and special education teachers. The chapters are collections of important topics requested by these professionals.

The book is to be used as a communication tool between the general physical education teacher and the paraeducator. This book will give paraeducators a better understanding of the discipline and purpose of physical education, their roles and responsibilities within physical education, communication and collaboration strategies, behavior management, instructional strategies, assessment, and IEP development and implementation. Furthermore, the resources included in this book will give more information about specific needs and interests within the physical education class and beyond.

A unique feature of this book is that it is written in understandable terminology for the professional who is not primarily trained in physical education. Each chapter includes understandable examples of each topic as well as tables, sidebars, and photos. In addition, each chapter was written by a higher education professional and a practitioner to ensure authenticity of information. This book also comes with a CD-ROM with handouts of each chapter and appendix as well as Microsoft PowerPoint® slides to assist in instructing paraeducators.

The first chapter, What is Physical Education?, reviews the purpose and importance of the discipline of physical education. It describes the role of the paraeducator in physical education. It also describes inclusion and its intended purpose. Finally, it discusses the legal term *least restrictive environment*.

Chapter 2, The Paraeducator's Roles and Responsibilities in Physical Education, outlines the various roles that the paraeducator can play in physical education classes. This chapter helps clarify what roles are the paraeducator's and what roles are solely the teacher's. It also clarifies duties of the paraeducator before, during, and outside of the class.

The third chapter, Paraeducator–Teacher Relationships: Creating Positive Environments, discusses communication and collaboration strategies to enhance the learning environment. This chapter gives suggestions for conflict resolution among professionals when relationships are strained. It also discusses the development of a learning community by continuing a caring approach to teaching and constructing an emotionally safe learning environment.

Chapter 4, Positive Methods for Dealing With Difficult Behavior, is an invaluable chapter on creating a positive space and the problems with punishment in today's classes. It discusses positive behavioral support and a skill-building approach to dealing with difficult behavior as well as social skills that can replace inappropriate behaviors.

Chapter 5, Instruction Strategies, reviews adaptations and modifications for different disabilities, as well as teaching strategies, peer tutoring, and training of peer tutors. This is invaluable information when the paraeducator is working in an inclusive setting.

Chapter 6, Assessment, addresses what assessment is and the purposes of assessment. It discusses the role of the paraeducator in the assessment process and various strategies for collecting assessment data.

Chapter 7, Individual Education Programs, reviews steps in the IEP process and the paraeducator's role in IEP development and implementation. Community-based programming relating to the IEP is reviewed as well as transition programming for adolescents.

Last, the appendixes provide abundant information on paraeducator responsibilities, various disabilities, special education acronyms, physical education terminology, ways to increase physical activity outside of the classroom, adapted aquatics, lifting and transferring students, first aid, ways to praise students, and confidentiality. It even has a section on professional preparation programs in adapted physical education for paraeducators who feel passionate enough in the area of adapted physical education to earn an advanced degree.

The authors hope that with this book, paraeducators will be empowered to become actively involved in physical education. This book will assist them in further advocating for themselves and their students, and with this support they can lead their students to healthy and active lifestyles. It is also our hope that paraeducators will use this book to empower all students with the knowledge that anything is possible and that hopes and goals can be achieved through understanding, cooperation, and creativity.

How to Use the CD-ROM

System Requirements

You can use this CD-ROM on either a Windows®-based PC or a Macintosh computer.

Windows®

- IBM PC compatible with Pentium® processor
- Windows® 98/2000/XP (2000 or XP recommended)
- Adobe Reader® 8.0
- Microsoft® PowerPoint® Viewer 2003 (included)
- 4x CD-ROM drive

Macintosh®

- Power Mac® required
- System 10.4 or higher
- 16 MB RAM (32 MB recommended)
- Adobe Reader® 8.0
- Microsoft® PowerPoint® Viewer OS9 or Viewer OS10 (included)
- 4x CD-ROM drive (or faster)

User Instructions

Windows

1. Insert the *Paraeducators in Physical Education CD-ROM*. (Note: The CD-ROM must be present in the drive at all times.)
2. Select the "My Computer" icon from the desktop.
3. Select the CD-ROM drive.
4. Open the "Contents.pdf" file.

Macintosh

1. Insert the *Paraeducators in Physical Education CD-ROM*. (Note: The CD-ROM must be present in the drive at all times.)
2. Double-click the CD icon located on the desktop.
3. Open the "Contents.pdf" file.

For customer support, contact Technical Support:

Phone: 217-351-5076 Monday through Friday (excluding holidays) between 7:00 a.m. and 7:00 p.m. (CST)

Fax: 217-351-2674

E-mail: support@hkusa.com

Acknowledgments

I gratefully acknowledge the writing team for their inspiration, professionalism, and dedication toward completing this wonderful project. My sincere appreciation goes to Sherry Folsom-Meek for her guidance and assistance with chapter 5. A very special thank-you is extended to Dr. Lauren Lieberman for her inspiration and infectious attitude toward life and the pursuit of excellence for all children. And last, I extend my heartfelt gratitude to my wife, Jill, for her love, constant support, and words of encouragement.

Rocco Aiello

I would like to thank my students and teachers, paraeducators, and learners with disabilities who allowed me to photograph them in real-life teaching situations, our adapted aquatics class. I would like to dedicate the small portion of the book that I wrote to my late daughter, Patricia Meek, who taught me a great deal about people with disabilities.

Dr. Sherry L. Folsom-Meek

I would like to thank two wonderful paraeducators who have helped to pioneer positions assisting in physical education, Deborah and Lisa. Their energy and enthusiasm have allowed for an expansion of creative and successful physical education opportunities for students with disabilities. Of course, I thank my supportive family, encouraging colleagues, and forever-inspiring students!

Jayne Glidewell

I would like to acknowledge my students and how they inspire me to be the best teacher I can

be. I would like to thank my colleagues, Scott Modell and Lauren Lieberman, for giving me the opportunity to work with such a great group of people and be part of such an important project to the field of physical education. Last but not least, I would like to thank my parents for all their support through school, athletics, and life—I love you both.

Ileah Jackson

Special thanks to Nadine Cain Laznovsky, Half Hollow Hills School District, and Barbara DeGere, Northport School District, for their feedback and help on this project. Your assistance was invaluable!

Dr. Ellen Kowalski

First, I would like to thank all the paraeducators from the Perkins School for the Blind and those I have worked with over the years for all I have learned from you! I would like to thank Kameron Maurer for his initial research on paraeducators. His efforts and energy led to my interest in this topic as a way to assist physical educators and the children with disabilities they work with. A huge thank you to Dr. Janet Seaman from the American Association for Physical Activity and Recreation (AAPAR) for her unending support in the entire process of this book. We could not have done it without you! I would like to thank all the contributors to this book. They shared their expertise, worked extremely hard, met deadlines, and believed in the project! I would like to thank Bonnie Pettifor and Kathleen Bernard from Human Kinetics for their creativity, focus, and encouragement in the editorial process. Lastly, I would like to thank my mother, Dr. Janet Joseph, for her support and encouragement through every part of my life. She was truly an inspiration to us all.

Dr. Lauren J. Lieberman

I would like to thank all the paraeducators I have worked with in the past and all those who assisted in the preparation of this book. You are the life force of special education.

Dr. Rebecca Lytle

I would like to acknowledge the City of Sacramento, Department of Parks and Recreation, Access Leisure Section for their work in supporting and acting as lead agency for numerous quality sport programs for individuals with disabilities. Specifically, I would like to thank Annie Desalernos for her tireless efforts and dedication to the quality of life of literally thousands of individuals with disabilities. Finally, I would like to acknowledge all of the students with disabilities whom I have worked with over the past 10 years. Your energy, spirit, and passion are inspiring.

Dr. Scott Modell

I would like to thank Dr. Lauren Lieberman. Without her support, dedication, and hard work, our field would not be as strong as it is today. She has been and continues to be a tremendous influence on me and my work. I would also like to thank all the paraprofessionals at School #29 for all of their efforts and the support they provide to me and our students not only in physical education but throughout the entire school day.

Carin Mulawka

To my husband, Dave, and my children Kevin, Katie, and Michael and his wife, Devon, I extend my love, gratitude, and appreciation for the wonderful life you have given me. And I can't wait until August for the arrival of our first grandchild.

Dr. Carol Ryan

A special thank-you to Monica Lepore from West Chester University for her contribution on aquatics in appendix F and to Mary Ellis for her contribution on confidentiality in appendix J.

CHAPTER 1

What Is Physical Education?

Rebecca Lytle and Jayne Glidewell

Guiding Questions

▶ What is the discipline of physical education?

▶ Why is physical activity important?

▶ What is the purpose of physical education across the life span?

▶ What is the role of the paraeducator in physical education classes?

▶ What are the benefits of inclusion for students with disabilities?

DURING a general physical education swim unit at a high school, students with disabilities were included with the assistance of their paraeducator. Each day of the week, the class had a different swim activity. On lap day, all students were trying to achieve a better score than the week before. Two students receiving adapted physical education within the general physical education class were wearing AquaJogger buoyancy belts to build confidence in their swimming abilities and to encourage lap-day participation. However, they were the only students in that class wearing the belts. After encouragement from the teacher, paraeducator, and other students, the belts came off within 2 weeks. This was a huge accomplishment. After years of unsuccessful attempts to swim on their own with their families, the students were swimming without help and recording 20 laps on lap day by the end of the unit. One mother was in tears when notified of the breakthrough, and the entire class celebrated.

Introduction

Success stories such as the previous one have not always been the norm for students with disabilities. Historically, children with disabilities have often been shunned, left in orphanages, or abandoned to die. Fortunately, attitudes and perceptions have changed over the past several decades; however, it has not been an easy road to equal access in education for children with disabilities in the United States. It was not long ago that medical professionals told parents of children with disabilities that they should consider placing their child in an institution. They could then put the experience of having a child with a disability behind them and start a fresh life without the so-called burden of raising a child with a disability.

However, in 1975 the passage of the Education for All Handicapped Children Act (now known as the Individuals with Disabilities Education Act or IDEA, revised most recently in 1997) changed the face of education for all children, both those with and without disabilities. Gradually, students with disabilities have become part of the general physical education classroom. IDEA requires that all children, regardless of disability, be provided with free, appropriate public education. IDEA also stipulates that all children, regardless of abilities, be educated with their peers without disabilities to the maximum extent appropriate (Federal Register, 1999). Since the passage of this law, students with disabilities have gradually become integrated into the general education and physical education environments.

As programming for students with disabilities has shifted from segregated to more integrated physical education programs, the need for quality paraeducators to support students in these environments has increased. The importance of the paraeducator as a member of the special education team continues to grow as more and more children with disabilities are identified and teaching responsibilities increase in physical education. The paraeducator often knows the student better than any other professional and serves as an advocate and critical contact for educators and the student within the educational program. The role of paraeducators in physical education is to assist in providing every student with the opportunity to learn, meaningful content, and appropriate instruction (National Association for Sport and Physical Education [NASPE], 2004). Paraeducators play a significant role in providing all students with the opportunity to participate in quality physical education and helping students with disabilities become active and healthy for life.

IT was the first day that the adapted physical education students were included in the general physical education class. The first thing they had to do was to dress out. The adapted physical education specialist had gone over each student's goals and individual needs (as well as disabilities) with Laticia, the paraeducator, so she felt confident that all would go as planned. However, that was not to be the case.

Laticia had the responsibility to oversee three girls in the locker room. Two of the students were supposed to be independent and had participated in junior high physical education. They were freshmen, though, and in a new setting, and they seemed very much in need of assistance. The other student had autism and was uncomfortable in the loud, chaotic locker room. While Laticia was assisting the other two students, she wandered out of the area. Laticia almost lost her! So the first few minutes of class were a little rough. Laticia decided to see if the two girls could make it on their own (with minor assistance from other girls in the class). To her surprise, they did. Meanwhile she took the student with autism for a walk and they reentered the locker room after everyone else had left. This turned out to be a great idea. The student dressed out that day, just a little late. Sometimes plan A doesn't work and quick decisions need to be made. That day, Laticia felt she made the right choice to just slow down. The joy of the job can be the unexpected challenges that turn out just fine!

The special education team consists of all the people who support a child. This includes IEP (i.e., individualized educational program) team members (parent, administrator, special education teacher, general education teacher, physical education teacher, and individuals who have completed assessments) as well as other critical individuals such as the paraeducator, bus driver, school support staff, and others who interact with the child during the day.

What Is Physical Education?

Physical education is defined in IDEA as the development of physical and motor fitness; fundamental motor skills and patterns; and skills in aquatics, dance, and individual and group games and sports (including intramural and lifetime sports). See table 1.1 for details on each component.

Although this is the definition under special education law, it parallels the expectation for all individuals. The current national standards for physical education (NASPE, 2004, p. 11) identify a physically educated person as meeting the following six standards:

- Demonstrates competency in motor skills and movement patterns needed to perform a variety of physical activities.

- Demonstrates understanding of movement concepts, principles, strategies, and tactics as they apply to the learning and performance of physical activity.

- Participates regularly in physical activity.

- Achieves and maintains a health-enhancing level of physical fitness.

▶ TABLE 1.1 Definition of Physical Education	
Components	**Definition**
Physical fitness	Refers to the development of health-related fitness (e.g., cardiovascular endurance, body composition, flexibility, muscular strength, muscular endurance).
Motor fitness	Refers to skill-related fitness (e.g., agility, balance, coordination, power, speed, reaction time).
Fundamental patterns	Divided into locomotor patterns (e.g., walking, running, jumping, galloping, hopping, skipping) and nonlocomotor patterns (e.g., throwing, catching, striking, kicking, punting).
Aquatics	Involves swimming using various strokes, water exercise, or hydrotherapy goals (i.e., increasing range of motion).
Dance and rhythms	Involves repeating an action or movement with regularity and in time to a particular pattern.
Individual games	Involves sports with no more than one or two players (e.g., archery, badminton, golf, tennis).
Team sports	Involves sports with more than three players per side (e.g., basketball, baseball, football, rugby).

- Exhibits responsible personal and social behavior that respects self and others in physical activity settings.
- Values physical activity for health, enjoyment, challenge, self-expression, and social interaction.

These standards apply to all students, regardless of their abilities. However, how a child exhibits these standards may vary from one child to another. For example, one student might enjoy riding a bicycle on a daily basis or participating in a soccer league, while another might enjoy pushing a racing wheelchair through the park after school or playing wheelchair basketball. Each is participating regularly in physical activity based on personal interests and desires. Within schools, this means providing students with consistent programs to teach them the skills necessary to be lifelong participants in physical activity.

The content presented to children in kindergarten will certainly be different from that presented to high school students. For example, the first standard states, "Demonstrates competency in motor skills and movement patterns needed to perform a variety of physical activities." For the kindergartener this might include such basic skills as jumping, hopping, galloping, catching a bounced ball, or discovering the ability to balance on different body parts. For the high school student, the standard would be met by learning more refined skills and applying them in an activity. Examples include volleyball passing, swimming strokes such as freestyle or the breaststroke, dance sequences, and selecting the appropriate club for a stroke in golf. At the high school level, students should be able to combine and sequence skills appropriately to participate in complex games, sports, aquatics, dance, or outdoor pursuits (NASPE, 2004).

Why Is Physical Education Important?

Human beings are designed for movement. Without it, the muscles deteriorate and the body's ability to function begins to fail. Yet current trends in the United States continue to point to declines in physical activity and an increase in childhood obesity and diabetes. Since 1963, incidence of childhood obesity has risen from 4% to 11% and continues to rise (USDHHS, 2004). Some lifelong benefits of physical activity include lower blood pressure and reduced risk for stroke, coronary heart disease, colon cancer, and diabetes, as well as reduced swelling and pain associated with arthritis. Physical activity also assists in weight control; contributes to healthy bones, muscles, and joints; and increases strength, stamina, flexibility, and an overall sense of well-being (Centers for Disease Control and Prevention [CDC], 2004). Exercise for individuals with disabilities may be even more critical since they are at greater risk for a sedentary lifestyle and exercise can help improve circulation, digestion, balance, range of motion, and many other factors related to activities of daily living and general mobility. Appendix I, Ideas for Increasing Physical Activity, describes specific ways the paraeducator can help promote physical activity throughout the day for students with disabilities.

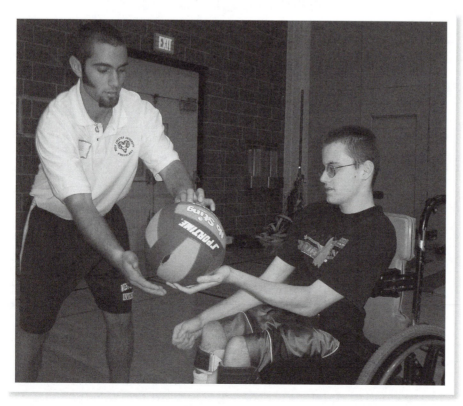

▶ Assisting a student with athletic skills, such as serving in volleyball, can help the student to want to engage regularly in physical activity.

The U.S. Surgeon General's Report on Physical Activity and Health (1996) reported that people with disabilities engage in approximately 10% less physical activity than people without disabilities (27.2% to 37.4%), yet the benefits of physical activity for all individuals is clear.

What Is the Purpose of Physical Education?

The purpose of physical education is to "help students develop the skills, knowledge and desires they need in order to be physically active now and for the rest of their lives" (Himberg, 2004). When working with students with disabilities, this means identifying skills needed to participate with their peers throughout their school experience and in the community as adults. Physical education changes across the life span the same as any other curriculum content area. For example, in kindergarten a student learns the alphabet and then begins to put the letters together to make words. Once this is accomplished, sentences can be made and eventually entire books can be read. As the student ages, the complexity of vocabulary and grammar increases. Finally, as an adult, the student can choose specific reading material for learning and leisure. The same is true for physical education. The student begins by learning individual skills such as standing, walking, or jumping. These skills are then combined into simple games or activities. Later, the student can use these skills in more complex tasks and sports, and as an adult, in physical activities chosen for lifetime enjoyment, pleasure, and health benefits. Table 1.2 illustrates the general content of development across the school years.

Many people had negative experiences in physical education as a child. You may remember yourself or a peer being picked last for a team or always being knocked out first in dodgeball. These types of experiences are not appropriate for anyone and do not represent what the discipline of physical education is all about. As a paraeducator, you can play an important role in ensuring that students with disabilities are not subject to such inappropriate practices as elimination games, students picking teams, or exercise as punishment.

Such practices negatively affect students of all abilities as well as those with a disability. The Web site of Concerned Adults and Students for Physical Education Reform (CASPER) has many great suggestions for appropriate practices that can support you as a concerned adult working with students with disabilities in the physical education setting (www.csuchico.edu/casper).

Preschool

The National Association for Sport and Physical Education (NASPE) has recently published a document titled *Active Start* (NASPE, 2002). This document provides guidelines for appropriate programming for students from birth to 5 years of age. Specific guidelines for preschool include the following:

Guideline 1: Preschoolers should accumulate at least 60 minutes daily of structured physical activity.

Guideline 2: Preschoolers should engage in at least 60 minutes and up to several hours

▶ **TABLE 1.2 General Content Areas Across the Public School Age Span**

Early childhood (preschool)	Elementary school	Secondary school into early adulthood
• Fundamental motor skills	• Locomotor skills	• Sport-related skills
• Orientation skills	• Nonlocomotor skills	• Health-related fitness
• Play participation	• Object-control skills	• Lifetime activities
• Locomotor skills	• Movement concepts	• Aquatics
• Object control	• Dance and rhythms	• Activities of daily living
• Water readiness	• Aquatics	
	• Fitness	
	• Leisure activities	

of daily, unstructured physical activity and should not be sedentary for more than 60 minutes at a time except when sleeping.

Guideline 3: Preschoolers should develop competence in movement skills that are building blocks for more complex movement tasks.

Guideline 4: Preschoolers should have indoor and outdoor areas that meet or exceed recommended safety standards for performing large-muscle activities.

Guideline 5: Individuals responsible for the well-being of preschoolers should be aware of the importance of physical activity and facilitate the children's movement skills.

▶ It is important for paraeducators and teachers to engage students in physical activity at young ages so that it can become a lifelong habit.

Students at this age should begin to learn basic locomotor skills such as walking, running, jumping, hopping, leaping, sliding, and galloping. In addition, they should be learning basic object-control skills, such as throwing, catching, and striking, as well as playground participation. Playground skills include swinging, tricycle riding, climbing a ladder and going down the slide, and so on. Students typically learn these skills individually or within a small group. Instruction is usually child directed and is facilitated by the teacher or paraeducator. Group instruction frequently includes imaginative play, play centers or stations, and a thematic approach to instruction.

Elementary School

At the elementary age, students begin to refine their fundamental motor skills and apply different movement concepts to skills such as those listed in table 1.3. Skill themes include locomotor, nonlocomotor, and manipulative skills. Locomotor skills involve the movement of the body from one place to another across a space, whereas nonlocomotor skills are movements performed with the body while staying in one place, such as twisting and bending. Manipulative skills include receiving an object or projecting an object into space such as catching, throwing, or kicking. We use these skill themes in some capacity in everything we do. For example, when a paraeducator takes students to physical education, they are all using a locomotor skill in walking to get to class. When the students participate in a basketball unit, they are walking, running, sliding, catching, throwing, jumping, and so on as they participate in the game.

In addition, we modify these skills using movement concepts in order to improve or change how we perform a skill. Movement concepts include space awareness, effort, and relationships. Space awareness is the ability to know where the body is in space and includes a person's location, directions, levels, extensions (e.g., tennis racket, golf club), and the pathways used as one moves through space. Effort qualities of movement include time, force, and flow. Relationships include the position of the body in relation to the self, objects, or others. Table 1.3 provides a complete list of skill themes and movement concepts.

Examples of how students combine skill themes with movement concepts include running with changes in speed (fast and slow) and direction (forward, backward, right, or left) or throwing at different levels (high, medium, or low) with a partner. Students also should begin putting skills together such as dribbling and passing to a partner or performing a simple dance sequence.

Paraeducators can help students with disabilities achieve their physical education IEP goals and

TABLE 1.3 Skill Themes and Movement Concepts

SKILL THEMES

Locomotor skills	Nonmanipulative skills	Manipulative skills
Walking	Turning	Throwing
Running	Twisting	Catching
Leaping	Rolling	Dribbling
Hopping	Balancing	Kicking
Skipping	Transferring weight	Volleying
Galloping	Stretching	Punting
Sliding	Curling	Striking with short implements
Chasing, fleeing, dodging	Jumping and landing	Striking with long implements

MOVEMENT CONCEPTS

Space awareness	Effort	Relationships
Location: self-space, general space	Time: fast, slow, sudden, sustained	Of body parts: round, narrow, wide, twisted, symmetrical, asymmetrical
Directions: up, down, forward, backward, right, left, clockwise, counterclockwise	Force: strong, light	With objects or people: over and under, on, off, near, far, in front, behind, along, through, meeting, parting, surrounding, alongside
Levels: low, middle, high	Flow: bound, free	With people: leading, following, mirroring, matching, unison, contrast, alone in a mass, solo, partners, groups, between groups
Pathways: straight, curved, zigzag		
Extensions: large, small, near, far		

Reprinted from G.M Graham, S.A. Holt/Hale, and M.A. Parker, 2004, *Children moving: A reflective approach to teaching physical education* (New York, McGraw-Hill Companies). With permission of The McGraw-Hill Companies.

objectives (see chapter 7) by helping students develop their movement skills within the context of physical education class and assisting with modifications as needed. These modifications should be determined with the general or adapted physical education teacher. For example, Ming uses a wheelchair and her class is working on throwing and catching with tennis balls. Ming has trouble maintaining control of the ball. For this reason she uses a modification. Her adapted physical education teacher has placed a Velcro mat on her lap tray to help her maintain control of the ball when she traps it in her lap. The Velcro prevents the ball from slipping off her lap so that she can pick it up and throw it back to her partner.

Secondary School

Once students have mastered skill themes and movement concepts and have begun to use them in more dynamic environments, they are ready to apply their skills in more formalized activities. These may include individual, dual, and team sports; aquatics; social and cultural dance; self-defense; gymnastics; and outdoors pursuits and challenges. Students at this level should not only know the rules for game play but also understand training principles for skills and strategies that improve game play. Students are learning to self-assess, set goals, and improve their skills independently. The major focus in programs should be learning and applying skills rather than, for example, competitive game play all the time. For example, students should learn how to hit a cross court forehand and cross court backhand and when to use them before they play a competitive tennis game (Himberg, Hutchinson, & Roussell, 2003). Students should be learning to interact cooperatively with others, demonstrate respect, and build positive self-esteem through engagement with individuals with varying abilities, skills, and interests.

Finally, students should know and understand the components of health-related fitness and be able to set personal fitness goals to maintain a healthy lifestyle. As students transition to adulthood, they should be able to identify activities appropriate for their needs based on their individual capabilities, interests, needs, and resources to participate in lifetime activities (NASPE, 2004). Paraeducators play a critical role at this level of development and can assist in the development of greater independence, setting personal goals for skill improvement as well as fostering cooperation and respect among students. In addition, paraeducators often play an important part in transition activities in the community and can serve as a wonderful role model for students as they begin to participate in activities within the community such as aerobics, weight training, cross-country skiing, or swimming.

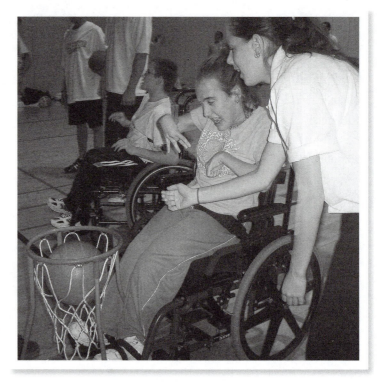

▶ Paraeducators should support students in their physical activities so that they can participate in activities with all types of students.

What Is Inclusion?

ONE day at the grocery store, Ben was shopping with his mom. He passed Sally in the vegetable department and said hello. Ben explained to his mom that Sally was on his volleyball team in his physical education class. Given Sally's obvious challenges, Ben's mother questioned Ben as to how she could play. Ben replied that Sally was allowed to serve from the 10-foot (3-meter) line and she usually scored points for the team. Ben was also proud of the fact that he helped Sally learn how to receive a serve. The next day, Sally's mom mentioned to the paraeducator and physical education teacher how neat it was for Sally to be recognized outside of school by one of her peers without disabilities.

In an effort to define inclusion, it is best to first define a least restrictive environment. This is the requirement by federal law that students with disabilities receive their education, to the maximum extent appropriate, with peers without disabilities and that students receiving special education are not removed from general classes unless, even with supplemental aides and services, education in regular classes cannot be achieved satisfactorily (www.specialedprep.net/integration.htm).

The term *inclusion* reflects a philosophy in which all students, regardless of abilities or disabilities, are educated in the same environment—an environment in which each student's individual needs are met (Block, 2007). It goes beyond simply physically placing a student in a general education classroom. "An inclusive school (or setting) is a place where everyone belongs, is accepted, and is supported by his or her peers and other members of the school community in the course of having his or her educational needs met" (Stainback & Stainback, 1990, p. 3). Embedded within this definition is the understanding that students with disabilities will still receive an individually determined program with supplementary services and supports to meet their unique needs (Block, 2007).

In terms of physical education services, this means that individually determined goals, benchmarks, and accommodations are provided within the general physical education environment by staff members who are trained to provide these services (e.g., adapted physical education specialist, trained general physical education teacher, trained adapted physical education paraeducator, or trained peer tutor) rather than outside of the classroom by taking the child to special services.

According to the Council for Exceptional Children (CEC), inclusion is

- providing the most appropriate education for each student in the least restrictive environment,
- placing students based on assessed educational needs rather than clinical labels,
- providing support services to general educators so they can effectively serve students with disabilities in the general environment, and
- uniting general and special education to help students with disabilities to have equal educational opportunities.

Inclusion is not

- dumping students with disabilities into general classes without the support and services they need to be successful,
- trading the quality of a student's education for integration or necessary intensive support services,
- doing away with or cutting back on special education services,
- ignoring each student's unique needs,
- students having to learn the same thing at the same time in the same way,
- expecting general education teachers to teach students who have disabilities without the support they need to teach all students effectively, or
- sacrificing the education of general education students so that students with disabilities can be integrated.

As a result of IDEA, general physical education teachers have had to become familiar with terms and concepts in special education, and they often take an active role in the IEP process (see chapter 7). Many general physical educators identify limited awareness and support as the major reason for their resistance to including students with disabilities in their classes. This limited awareness and

support includes the following areas (California Department of Education, 2001, p. 79):

- Student's legal right to a free appropriate public education (FAPE)
- General educator's responsibilities to each student
- Accommodations and modifications available to the general educator when working with a particular student with a disability
- Student's disability and how to safely accommodate the student
- Forms of support and resources available
- District and site administrators' responsibilities to the students and the general educator and how to accommodate the students' needs and facilitate their success

Administrators, teachers, and support staff set the tone for successful inclusion. In many cases, paraeducators can help to increase the awareness of general physical education teachers in regard to special education. General physical education teachers and paraeducators can encourage students without disabilities to assist in the process by interacting in an acceptable manner with their peers with disabilities and by functioning as role models, peer tutors, advocates, and friends (Stainback & Stainback, 1990).

Specifically, in physical education, *inclusion* can be defined as an opportunity for students with disabilities to be with peers socially, to observe positive behavior modeling, and of course to develop fitness and physical skills. Inclusion can often produce higher expectations and surprising results. Inclusion also ensures equal opportunities for all students to access facilities and equipment. But, most importantly, it is a wonderful setting in which to develop a sense of community and compassion for the varying abilities of all students. Benefits of inclusion include the following:

- Increased social development
- Increased physical development
- Increased participation with peers
- Higher expectations for student performance
- Equal opportunities for facilities and equipment

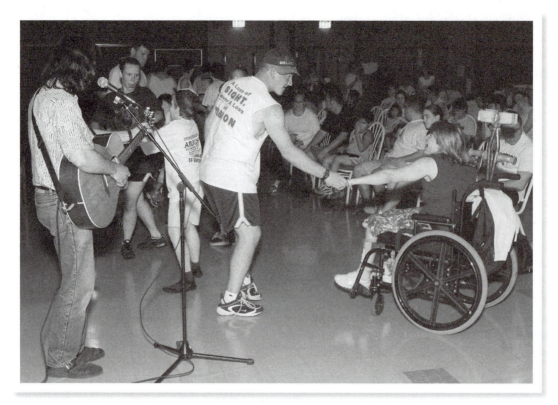

▶ Paraeducators are in a great position to facilitate interactions between students with and without disabilities.

- Sense of community, belonging, and compassion
- Appreciation of individual differences
- Development of friendships

Seaman, Depauw, Morton, and Omoto (2003) have said that "inclusion is more than a 'placement' it is an attitude." The expected attitude is one in which all people are treated with respect and value (Seaman et al., 2003). As a paraeducator, it is critical to help promote this positive philosophy regarding inclusion. It is the job of the adapted physical education specialist to initiate the placement, based on an IEP decision, and communicate student modifications, goals, and medical background to the general physical education teacher, but it is the paraeducator who will often be maintaining that relationship, continuing strong communication, and overseeing the spirit of community.

Inclusion can be accomplished in a variety of ways. It is only limited by your imagination. Although it is important that students with disabilities are included to the maximum extent possible, certain circumstances may prohibit participation. If it is determined that full inclusion is not appropriate, partial placement may be appropriate. For example, for students who are more challenged by behavior or overstimulation, it might make sense to include them during stretches or running activities only. Reverse mainstreaming is another option. This involves students without disabilities joining a program for students with disabilities. With the help of peer tutors and physical education partners, students without disabilities have been included in adapted physical education settings.

There is a continuum of placement options in which a student can receive any one or a combination of services. In some instances a paraeducator may assist a student throughout the day in all of the academic areas, including physical education. However, it is also possible that the student is able to participate in physical education without support services. The following list (Block, 2007) outlines the possible options for serving students with disabilities in physical education:

- Full-time general physical education teacher, no support needed

- Full-time general physical education teacher, accommodations needed (e.g., interpreter, adapted equipment, special instructions)

- Adapted physical education provided within the general physical education environment (student has unique goals and objectives as well as the need for special accommodations, but the goals and accommodations can be carried out within the general environment)

- Adapted physical education provided within the general physical education environment, with direct support from the adapted physical education specialist (specialist comes into the general environment to help students work on their unique goals and objectives and with special accommodations)

- Adapted physical education provided part time within general physical education and part time in separate class

- Adapted physical education provided full time in separate class in general school building

- Adapted physical education provided full time in separate class in a special school

- Adapted physical education provided full time in separate class at home, in a hospital, or in a treatment facility

In addition to these options, the IEP team determines what type of adapted physical education service is best for the student. This may include direct and collaborative consultative services in any of the previously mentioned settings. Although there can be challenges to including students with disabilities in classes with their peers without disabilities, the benefits and research supporting this service model far outweigh any potential negatives (Block, 2007).

Once the positive philosophy and attitudes have been established, the class itself needs to be designed. Preplanning for inclusion is crucial. Some schools have annual disability awareness days, and others invite guest speakers or have classroom discussions to promote an awareness and understanding of individual differences. As Seaman et al. (2003, p. 276) point out, "The most successful classes have been where a wide variety of learning activities and instructional strategies are used and students have the opportunity to make choices to meet their individual needs and preferences."

Paraeducators' Role in Physical Education

WITH minor modifications, such as a key lock, Suzie was able to dress out in the general physical education locker room. She had a 5-minute head start with her paraeducator so that she would be able to get to the exercise line on time. Suzie felt so much a part of the class and was very proud of herself. Although Suzie was unable to tie her shoes, her mom found some cool zip-up tennis shoes and Suzie was able to be independent in dressing and changing for physical education.

The early experiences students have in physical education and in recreational settings help shape their attitudes about activity for the rest of their lives. The paraeducator plays a critical role in ensuring positive and appropriate physical activity experiences for students with disabilities. For these reasons it is extremely important that paraeducators understand the benefits of physical activity and assist in promoting healthy lifestyles for the students they serve. How the paraeducator supports and assists a student with a disability is vital to the development of positive attitudes and competence in movement experiences. A study titled "Helping or Hovering? Effects of Instructional Assistant Proximity on Students with Disabilities" showed that instructional assistant proximity to students with disabilities could actually have a negative effect and result in many of the following concerns (Giangreco, Edelman, Luiselli, & MacFarland, 1997):

- Interference with general educators taking responsibility for teaching the child

- Separation from classmates

- Dependence on adults

- Reduced peer interactions

- Loss of personal control by the student

- Limitations on receiving competent instruction

- Interference with instruction of other students

However, with appropriate interactions the paraeducator can be instrumental in creating a successful learning environment for the student. Indeed, studies show that most paraeducators take their jobs seriously and are committed to assisting students (Auxter, Pyfer, & Huettig, 2005):

- Paraeducators assume an advocate role for including their students.
- They seek to make the experience positive for the general education teacher.
- They feel responsible for controlling all student behaviors to avoid disruption in the classroom.
- They believe they are a critical liaison among parents, the general education teacher, and other school personnel involved with the child.
- They believe themselves to be experts regarding the student to whom they are assigned.

Table 1.4 provides a variety of dos and don'ts for working with students with disabilities in the physical education setting with regard to fostering independence.

Summary

Paraeducators play an important role in supporting inclusion and participation of students with disabilities in physical education and ultimately in maintaining a healthy and active lifestyle. Understanding the goals and focus of a quality physical education program prepares paraeducators to ask purposeful questions of special education team members on how to best support the learning and independence of students with disabilities. As an advocate and liaison between professionals and the family, the paraeducator's knowledge, support, interest, and commitment to the student with a disability make the paraeducator a valuable member of the special education team.

Inclusion Success Stories

The remainder of this chapter is dedicated to specific benefits that support inclusion opportunities. These real-life stories (names have been changed to maintain anonymity) demonstrate that inclusion is more than a model for special education service

▶ TABLE 1.4 Dos and Don'ts: Real Paraeducators Aren't Babysitters	
Dos: The helping paraeducator	**Don'ts: The hindering paraeducator**
Assists only as the student needs it. Makes modifications so the student can do the task independently or with minimal assistance.	Babysits or watches without assisting when needed, or may not know how to assist. Could also be overly helpful.
Assists other students in the class who need help.	Sits in the environment where the student is and just watches.
Moves away from the student to encourage independence as appropriate.	Always sits or stands right next to the student.
Finds ways to encourage social interactions between students with and without disabilities.	Serves as a physical presence and barrier for communication with other students or the general education teacher.
Encourages the general education teacher to interact with the student within the context of the physical education class, including instruction and feedback when appropriate.	Gives all the instruction and feedback to the student without encouraging teacher or peer interaction.
Allows the student to talk for self and encourages communication directly with the student from others.	Talks for the student.
Provides appropriate, positive, specific feedback or corrective feedback as needed.	Allows the student to continue to practice incorrectly.
Values the student's interests and desires and utilizes this information in interactions and modifications for instruction.	Assists the student based on own ideas about what the student needs without regard for the student's interests.

delivery. "It is a new paradigm for thinking and acting in ways that include all persons in a society where diversity is becoming the norm rather than the exception. Our schools and communities will become as good as we decide to make them" (Stainback & Stainback, 1996, p. 11).

Adapted Physical Education Students Want to Do What Other Students Are Doing

As difficult as it was for Tom to serve a badminton birdie, he wanted to be in the class badminton tournament. After lots of hard work and using a modified racket, Tom was finally getting his serve in consistently. However, he continued to struggle with the rallies, and the general physical education teacher was worried that the other students might not want Tom for their partner. The adapted physical education teacher suggested Tom play on a team of three and the problem was solved. Tom's team was very competitive.

Opportunity for Social Growth and Maturity

Tony was a student with a disability who was easily frustrated. He would have meltdowns that involved yelling, slamming doors, and sometimes crying. It was a risk to put him into an inclusive setting for physical education, but the IEP team decided to try it. The negative behaviors were never observed in the class. The educators believed that Tony didn't want to look different or draw attention to himself in the mix of the general student population. Even though he never mentioned his behavior, he surprised everyone.

Built-In Tolerance Lesson

The inclusion experience provides its own path for teachable moments. Sometimes when a student with disabilities makes incredible effort to perform a skill, it creates an awareness of personal strength in all students. Mary wanted to be in the all-school track meet, but there was a concern about her wheelchair getting in the way of the runners. The students had observed her working hard during physical education (just like they were) to prepare for the big event. Mary was very disappointed when told about the concerns. After some discussion and some student pressure, it was finally resolved that there would be a wheelchair division in the races and that the staff would round up wheelchairs for students without disabilities to use. Many students were eager to participate in this division; in fact, there were three wheelchair heats. And Mary took first in her heat.

Sport Fans Unite

At some time or other students may have the opportunity to watch one of their peers compete in an extracurricular sporting event. If students have an awareness of who is playing, it makes the game much more interesting. In addition, through participation in general physical education, a student with a disability may have the opportunity to actually experience playing team sports or learn a specific position on a team with peers. At a football game last year, Jorge, a student with a cognitive disability, remembered playing center in flag football during class. His only job on the field was to hike the ball, but he learned that skill well. When his sister took him to the game on a Friday night, not only did he recognize some classmates, but he also had a basic understanding of the game. At one point, he yelled out, "Hey, that's my position." According to his sister, his interest in the game was amazing. It was the first time she had taken him to a game that he actually paid attention to. Of course, he enjoyed the band too (as do we all).

CHAPTER 2

The Paraeducator's Roles and Responsibilities in Physical Education

Ronald Davis, Amy Oliver, and Cindy Piletic

Guiding Questions

▶ What is the status of the paraeducator in physical education?

▶ What are three of the paraeducator's responsibilities before, during, and after physical education class?

▶ What is the paraeducator's role in ensuring safety during physical education?

▶ What are four ways the paraeducator can communicate with the physical educator, special education classroom teacher, and related service personnel?

MR. Santos was a middle school general physical educator at Nixon Middle School in Muncie, Indiana. He had more than 20 years experience in teaching physical education but had never taught students with disabilities in his classes. One year 12 students from two classes who were considered severely disabled were assigned to Mr. Santos for physical education. In order to successfully provide programming, he sought input from the classroom teachers and a local university professional in adapted physical education, Dr. Wheel. Together these professionals developed a strategy to utilize the students' paraeducators assigned for classroom instruction in physical education. Three planning meetings took place to map out a method of utilizing the paraeducators. The classroom teachers, Ms. Bell and Mrs. Green, agreed that the paraeducators would be responsible for transitioning the students to the gym and getting them ready for the class. Once in the gymnasium, the paraeducators would help position the students on the gym floor in their starting formation and be ready to help implement the activities.

During the second and third planning meetings, Mr. Santos explained his plans for the next two units in physical education. From those discussions, modifications for the activities were discussed for each child with Ms. Bell and Mrs. Green. With input from Dr. Wheel, Mr. Santos developed a system of index cards with diagrams of the activities and modifications for the individual child on the cards. The index cards used simple diagrams and stick figures to show the paraeducators how to complete the activity. Only one activity was written on a card for a specific child. For example, one card might diagram a student moving through a series of cones while lying on a scooter using a zigzag pattern. With his index card system established, Mr. Santos was optimistic he could teach the students with disabilities in his physical education class.

Introduction

The role of paraeducators in physical education can be stated very simply. Their responsibility is to assist the physical education teacher through activity planning, implementation, and evaluation. The role of the paraeducator has changed as more and more students with disabilities have been included in the general education setting. Traditionally, paraeducators have assisted students with disabilities in the classroom, with no expectations of fulfilling these same responsibilities in the physical education setting. Many paraeducators consider physical education as their break time and fail to continue providing instructional support.

According to Doyle (1997), paraeducators believe they have been hired to assist the classroom teacher by implementing student behavior management plans, assisting with student assessments, helping to manage tasks associated with the IEP, and providing assistance with small- and large-group activities. Paraeducators have also provided assistance in the area of personal care for students, including assistance with restroom needs and assistance during wheelchair transfers (Giangreco, Broer, & Edelman, 2002; Giangreco & Doyle, 2002; Horton, 2001). These same responsibilities and others must be transferred to the physical education setting since school reform and inclusion appear to be here to stay.

This chapter will discuss the paraeducator's status with the professional in physical education; responsibilities before, during, and outside the physical education class; roles for ensuring safety in the physical education setting; and communication and collaboration links with specialists or related service personnel (i.e., physical and occupational therapists and the physical educator). Paraeducators should be considered equal to other professionals serving on a special education team. It is the contribution of the entire team that will provide appropriate programming in physical education for a student with a disability.

Status of Physical Educators

The paraeducator can bring a wealth of knowledge to the physical education class that can help the physical educator provide a quality program. Physical educators recognize that the paraeducator spends more time with the student throughout the day than they do. A paraeducator is considered to be working alongside a professional. They are there to assist, share their opinions, and contribute to the knowledge and insight about the student with a disability. All of this contributes to the educational learning environment, both in the classroom and in the gymnasium.

There should be general expectations for the paraeducator in a physical education setting. More specific responsibilities will be provided later in the chapter. Review table 2.1 to see what can be expected of paraeducators in a physical education setting. Use this table as a quick reference guide when working with students with disabilities in physical education.

The paraeducator is a member of a team working to develop appropriate programming for a student with a disability. Paraeducators and physical educators need to work together to identify and develop information regarding the student's behavior management program, medication needs, feeding programs, and learning cues or prompts. Some school systems might implement a physical education inclusion team, or PEIT (Block, 2007). The PEIT is composed of several professionals such as school district administrators, teachers, parents, and therapists. Paraeducators need to be part of that team. They can contribute to planning and implementing assessment, instruction, and reinforcement techniques. Physical educators are making every effort to use this knowledge and actively engage the paraprofessional as a partner while planning and implementing the student's activities. Physical educators want to utilize the paraeducator within numerous activities. Paraeducators' expertise could be used in positioning the student in a game or activity, interpreting

▶ TABLE 2.1 Expectations of Paraeducators in the Physical Education Setting

Responsibilities	General expectations
Have good working knowledge of student movement.	Have a good working knowledge of your student in a movement setting and outdoor environment. Students with disabilities may have reactions and limitations in activity-based settings that are not visible in the classroom environment. In addition, it is difficult for the teacher to remember information about all the students. For example, when going outdoors, a friendly reminder to the teacher that your student is allergic to bee stings can be helpful. Or, when the weather is warm, remind the teacher and your student with spina bifida about thermoregulation.
Learn terminology.	Learn general terminology related to movement and physical activity (e.g., dynamic balance, flexibility, target zone). This will help you to feel more comfortable in an active setting and to communicate more easily with the teachers and therapists who work with your student. If you don't understand terminology, these are good people to ask for help.
Know student's present level of performance (PLP).	Know your student's strengths and weaknesses described in the PLP and individual goals and objectives (see chapter 7) *before* you enter the gymnasium. When you understand these, you can better help your student work on the areas that need improvement in each activity.
Know the units for class.	Find out units of instruction and activity plans for the week before entering the gymnasium so that you can be ready to help your student maximize the physical education time.
Keep the physical educator up to date.	Keep the physical educator posted with up-to-date information about your student, such as if your student with autism had seizures yesterday, is having a bad day, or has been displaying poor eating and sleeping patterns. This is important so that the teacher can modify instruction to help the student still benefit from class.
Dress appropriately.	Dress appropriately for activity—wear comfortable clothing and sneakers. Be prepared to move with the student and get down on the gymnasium floor or grass. If you are wearing a skirt, dress slacks, or dress shoes, bring a change of clothes when your student has physical education.

When paraeducators work closely with the students, they become valuable sources of information as team members with high levels of knowledge of the students' needs and boundaries.

instruction for the student, or helping the student to safely engage in the activity. Although many of the paraeducator's responsibilities occur during the physical education class time, several roles can be fulfilled before and outside of each class.

Paraeducators' Responsibilities Before Physical Education Class

When a student physically moves from the classroom setting to the physical education setting, several events must take place. Preparation in the classroom before leaving for the gymnasium might include the following: putting books and papers away, transitioning through the hallways (which could require moving from the second floor of the building to the main floor), and waiting quietly to enter the gymnasium. Once at the gymnasium, students might have to line up at the door before entering or go to the locker room for changing and then move from the locker room into

▶ **TABLE 2.2   Responsibilities of Paraeducators Before Physical Education Class**

Environment	Activities	Paraeducator's role
Classroom	Preparation to go to gymnasium	Physically help the student store books, papers, or other material. Check for toileting concerns. Depending on the needs of the student, show pictures of the activities planned for the gymnasium to help the student make the transition. Physically help transfer the student to a wheelchair as needed.
Hallway	Movement in hallways, stairs, or elevators	Monitor speed and pace of movement in the hallway. Monitor noise level and behaviors. Continue communicating with the student to help reinforce the transition to the gymnasium (e.g., "We are going to work on our throwing and catching today like we did yesterday"). Perhaps use a picture or storyboard to assist with the transition. Help reinforce the starting position once in class by communicating the student's squad number or color.
Locker room or waiting area	Entering the locker room or waiting in the hallway to enter the gymnasium	Assist with changing clothes as needed. Minimal changing might include changing shoes or T-shirts. Continue to monitor noise level if waiting in the hallway.
Movement into the gym	Finding the starting position (i.e., squads, teams, or numbers on the floor)	If the physical educator uses a numbering system to line up or start the class, make sure that number is attached to the student's wheelchair as needed. If squads or teams are used, perhaps work with the physical educator to establish squads or teams using a color code. Make sure your student is not the last one into the gymnasium. Allow the student more time to view the environment before entering in order to help with the transition.

the gymnasium to assume their starting position (e.g., sitting in squads).

The paraeducator can assist with many of these preliminary activities and contribute to the learning readiness of the student with a disability. Table 2.2 provides examples of the responsibilities a paraeducator can fulfill before engaging in a physical education class.

Once inside the learning environment, the paraeducator's role must change. To better define the paraeducator's role during the physical education class, it is important to understand the difference between this environment and the classroom setting.

Paraeducators' Responsibilities During Physical Education

Paraeducators must realize that their role in a physical education class will require adjusting to differences in the environment compared with the regular classroom. Differences include a larger learning environment, larger pieces of equipment, more transitions within the setting, and generally more movement and noise. In order to better prepare for an encounter with this unique environment, paraeducators should understand certain phases that occur within a physical education class.

Block (2007) advocates that physical education teachers and paraeducators look at the class time in terms of phases of events or ecological encounters. These encounters or interactions can be recorded in what is referred to as an *ecological inventory*. An ecological inventory is an assessment of the student's interaction with the learning environment. The focus of this assessment is to gauge how the student with a disability interacts with various phases or encounters during a lesson. Assessment is not part of this chapter, but the phases in this

▶ TABLE 2.3	Suggested Responsibilities of Paraeducators During Phases of Physical Education Class	
Lesson phases	Student response	Paraeducator's role
Entering gym	Wait with classmates and move to designated location (i.e., squads or attendance lines).	Assist as needed. Provide verbal cues or physical assistance if the student uses a wheelchair. Keep the student focused, on task, and quiet.
Warm-up	Perform various warm-up activities (i.e., locomotor movement, flexibility, strength).	Assist movement around the gym as needed. Provide assistance with range of motion.
Instruction	Teacher provides teaching objectives for the day and activity format (i.e., stations and station rotation).	Help the student maintain a good position in class to clearly see and hear instructions. Help the student maintain attention. Repeat instructions as needed.
Transition to activity	Move to stations.	Consider logistics as needed (e.g., indoors versus outdoors). Prompt or inform the student that a transition is going to occur. If transition involves movement outdoors, routes need to be preplanned with teacher (e.g., consider surfaces to cross, distance, and time needed).
Performing skills	Perform skills as instructed, then rotate to next station	Assist the student with proper form for skills (e.g., kick, pass in soccer), then help with relocation to the next station.
Cool-down and wrap-up	Teacher provides feedback and might conduct brief relaxation or range-of-motion activity.	Make sure the student maintains a good position in class to see and hear clearly.
Transition back to classroom	Return to the classroom.	Consider the same movements and tasks necessary to transition to the activity.

discussion are examples of typical events occurring within a physical education class. These phases or events provide opportunities for paraeducators to assist general physical educators in furthering the educational experience of students with disabilities. In addition, the paraeducator can help the general physical educator adjust the amount of time spent with both groups of students so that the physical educator does not have to worry about overlooking anyone's needs. Table 2.3 describes events recorded in an ecological inventory within a typical physical education class and then offers suggestions for how the paraeducator can support that environment.

Paraeducators' Responsibilities Outside Physical Education Class

Not all of the paraeducator's responsibilities in physical education occur in the actual activity setting. Responsibilities outside of the gymnasium may include charting students' skills and behaviors, providing practice time on skill development during recess, checking homework related to phys-

ical education (e.g., bringing in pictures of athletes from magazines), or sharing ideas with the physical educator about learning opportunities that are occurring in the classroom. Such sharing sessions should be the result of scheduled meetings with the physical educator. Specific responsibilities of the paraeducator outside the physical education class are presented in table 2.4.

Safety in the Physical Education Setting

Safety for all students, especially those with disabilities, should be foremost in the mind of the physical educator. The paraeducator can greatly contribute to keeping the environment safe in the physical education class by monitoring activities, informing the teacher of dangerous environments, and modifying equipment usage. Table 2.5 describes specific examples of how the paraeducator can help the physical educator address safety for a student with a disability in physical education class.

▶ **TABLE 2.4   Suggested Responsibilities of Paraeducators Outside of Physical Education Class**

Activities outside physical education	Paraeducator's role
Reading aloud in class	Help the student read physical education and other sport material (e.g., *Sports Illustrated*) while helping to link the reading to activities learned in class.
Providing special help such as drilling with flash cards and spelling	Develop a card game using professional trading cards (e.g., baseball, basketball, or football) to help the student address social acceptance through sport opportunities.
	Develop flash cards for spelling movements or activities learned in physical education (e.g., *throw* or *kick* or *passing*).
	Combine spelling cards with trading cards to link similar activities from physical education class (e.g., *throw* with a professional football or baseball card).
Scoring objective tests and papers	Assist the physical educator by recording scores from fitness or motor tests.
Setting objectives with the teacher	Meet with the physical educator to discuss strengths and weaknesses of the student and how activities can be planned to address these issues.
Teaching instruction	Meet with the physical educator to discuss cues and prompts during instruction for the student.
	Share key words that will elicit the best student response.
	Teach the physical educator to use a student's word board.
	Develop a physical education picture board.

▶ Working with other team members both inside and outside of the classroom is important in facilitating the opportunity to share learning ideas with others and review students' progress.

▶ TABLE 2.5	Safety Responsibilities of Paraeducators in Physical Education
Activity	**Paraeducator's responsibility**
General monitoring of activity areas and medical safety concerns	Observe crowded playing conditions; maintain watch over inappropriate use of equipment (e.g., swinging of metal bats versus plastic bats, climbing on gymnastic equipment, jumping from inappropriate heights).
	Monitor the traffic pattern moving from one setting within the classroom to another (e.g., engaging in station work inside the gymnasium and then moving outdoors).
	Watch for side effects of medications; check helmets to be sure they are worn correctly.
	Use spray bottles during outdoor activities for students with heat intolerance (e.g., spinal cord quadriplegic).
Dangerous environments	Students should be monitored during throwing activities (e.g., chest- or bounce-pass relays during basketball units, target throwing activities, throwing and catching during softball units, kicking activities for soccer or kickball).
	Transfer students from wheelchairs to seated positions on the floor or double-wide scooters.
	Walk with students who are ambulatory during warm-up activities, any running events, or when movement occurs over uneven surfaces.
	Monitor students during forward rolling activities by ensuring the use of logrolling (e.g., for students with atlantoaxial instability).
Equipment modifications	Use leather-covered balls or cloth gloves for students who are latex hypersensitive.
	Show the physical educator how to walk with a student using a safety or gait belt for balance.

Communication With Specialists or Related Services

Related services are considered ancillary or support services for special education. The two services most closely associated with physical education are physical therapy (PT) and occupational therapy (OT). PTs work on large-muscle function such as standing up and walking, and OTs work on fine motor function such as eating, zipping up clothes, or buttoning. These two services assist with the educational program, including physical education, of a student with special needs. However, they should not be considered a replacement service for a physical education program. These services, which are put in place to help further the educational goals of the student with special needs, should not be considered direct services (i.e., physical education).

Many times a physical or occupational therapist will work in the special education classroom to improve a student's sitting posture, range of motion, trunk stability, fine motor control, eye–hand coordination, or other goals, thus assisting the student with learning. It is the paraeducator who frequently interacts with the specialist in this classroom environment as the two discuss the student's educational goals and objectives. The paraeducator and the PT and OT specialists share information about the student's attending behavior, specific seating positioning in a wheelchair or desk chair, appropriate pen or pencil grasp used for writing, or appropriate cueing to be used to gain the student's attention before instruction. The paraeducator should pass on this information to the physical educator. Table 2.6 mentions a few examples of information that should be shared with the physical educator by the paraeducator as developed by the PT and OT specialists.

Summary

The role of the paraeducator is changing within school systems. Paraeducators are being asked to contribute more assistance beyond clerical tasks (i.e., office assistance, filing, photocopying). Effective use of paraeducators by physical educators will require all professionals working together to recognize the paraeducator as a meaningful contributor to the students' program. The physical educator must use the paraeducator in roles before, during, and outside the classroom. Paraeducators can

▶ TABLE 2.6 Examples of Information Shared With PT and OT Specialists and Physical Educators	
Event or activity	**Enhancing communication between specialists and physical educator**
Changing in locker room for aquatics	Make sure a safe environment is established for changing. Place a wrestling mat or aerobics mat on the floor to provide a softer surface for transfer and changing. Work with the physical educator to demonstrate proper transfer techniques.
Providing hand-over-hand assistance or manual manipulation	Ensure proper placement of hands during manual manipulation for range-of-motion movement. Emphasize proper speed and control when manually moving a limb for range (e.g., do not move the limb too fast when working with a student with spastic cerebral palsy).
Positioning in wheelchair	Make sure to communicate proper seating position. Inspect and adjust strapping placement as needed. Check for abrasions and proper fit of straps and orthotics during activities. Help the physical educator reposition the student into the wheelchair after an activity is completed.
Transferring from wheelchair	Establish from the specialist that the student can work out of the wheelchair and convey that information to the physical educator. When considering a transfer out of the wheelchair, place a wrestling mat or aerobics mat on the floor to provide a softer surface for transfer.

help address safety concerns and serve to further the communication between school physical and occupational therapists and the physical educator. Clearly, defining the paraeducator's role within physical education, encouraging systematic and purposeful training programs, and creating an atmosphere of mutual respect for the paraeducators among all team members should have far-reaching benefits for all students, especially those with disabilities.

CHAPTER 3

Paraeducator–Teacher Relationships:

Creating Positive Environments

Scott Modell, Doug Collier, and Ileah Jackson

Guiding Questions

- ▶ How do active and reflective listening contribute to effective communication?

- ▶ What are some ways to communicate honestly and respectfully?

- ▶ What are the key concepts related to conflict resolution?

- ▶ How is an emotionally safe learning environment created?

M R. Rodriguez is a physical education teacher at Apollo Middle School and has been teaching for 6 years. He is very involved in his state organization and lectures several times each semester at the local university. He hosts student teachers each fall and feels as though he is a good teacher. The fall of his 7th year he had a student teacher, and he also had Ramaal, a 7th grader with autism. Mrs. O'Connell came with Ramaal to each class as his paraeducator. It was his first year in the school and her first year as his paraeducator. Mr. Rodriguez was happy she came to class and assumed she would help out with Ramaal during class, but Mrs. O'Connell sat on the crash mat and simply watched the class. Ramaal would often go off task and run out the door occasionally. Mrs. O'Connell often chased after him and brought him back, or the student teacher would redirect him, but he was disruptive and made it difficult for the class. Mr. Rodriguez became more and more frustrated with Mrs. O'Connell but did not say anything. Mrs. O'Connell was ready and willing to help in class but had no idea what to do. Finally, one day Ramaal knocked over half of an obstacle course that Mr. Rodriguez and the student teacher had set up, and he decided he'd had enough. He went to the principal's office and complained at length about Mrs. O'Connell. When the principal brought Mrs. O'Connell in, she said that she did everything she was asked to do in class. She was willing to do anything but was not asked to do anything, therefore creating a difficult and negative environment.

Introduction

As can be seen in the previous scenario, communication, collaboration, and teamwork from the start are invaluable to creating a successful educational environment for all. Efforts must be made by all parties in order to be clear and understand expectations. This chapter lays out positive ways to communicate and collaborate as a team.

Importance of Communication, Collaboration, and Teamwork

A variety of responsibilities are assigned to the paraeducator depending upon the physical classroom environment, the skill level of the paraeducator, the needs of the students, and the needs of the teacher. Regardless of your responsibilities, open communication, collaboration, and teamwork are critical in creating a successful learning environment for students with disabilities. The paraeducator is a key member of the special education team and has unique roles and responsibilities that must be clearly articulated to all team members.

As a team member, you should receive information on your roles and responsibilities from the teacher; this is part of the teacher's responsibility. Many teachers may initially be consumed with planning and providing lessons, so they may put off or forget to communicate your roles and responsibilities to you. You can take an active role by opening lines of communication early in the

▶ After communicating with the teacher, the paraeducator can move forward confidently regarding how to best work with the students.

semester so that information is shared in a timely and appropriate manner. In addition, communication skills and experiences of teachers vary, but once you open lines of communication, this should not be a problem since the teacher will recognize that your membership on the special education team is vital to the success of the students.

According to Sherrill (2004), people who like and respect each other tend to communicate better. Communication requires active listening and reflective listening. Active listening includes appropriate eye contact (looking people in the eyes when they are speaking to you), nodding your head (informing the speaker that you are paying attention), and positive verbal responses (e.g., "Okay" and "Uh-huh"). Reflective listening involves restating the speaker's ideas in summary form. This sends a message to the speaker that the message is important and is being attended to. Reflective listening encourages speakers to continue, allowing for more depth and substance to the communication (Sherrill, 2004).

It is also important to avoid negative nonverbal body language (e.g., lack of eye contact, frowning, folding your arms, looking at your watch). This may hinder communication by implying that you do not wish to be part of the communication process. Using active and reflective listening and avoiding negative nonverbal body language will help you create efficient, effective lines of communication, ensuring that each member of the special education team is involved and valued.

Setting aside time for collaborative meetings is a critical component of open and effective communication. Understandably, finding time can be difficult. Research suggests that time is a major barrier to effective collaboration (Karge, McClure, & Patton, 1995; Lytle & Collier, 2002). It is important to not let time be a barrier in your quest for effective communication. Some schools outline specific days of the week to meet for collaboration, while others designate a day or two each month. Time can vary from school to school and from classroom to classroom but should always be based on the needs of the students, teachers, and paraeducators. Some physical education teachers may wish to meet with the paraeducators before the beginning of each class, whereas others may prefer to meet at the beginning of each unit. In some schools there is not enough time between

▷ Adapted physical education teachers and paraeducators can schedule time to review class activities and lesson responsibilities far in advance, or that review session can happen right before class time.

classes for a meeting. Again, the specific needs of the teacher, paraeducator, and student will dictate the frequency of meetings. Whatever the structure of your school, it is important to set aside some time for collaborative meetings.

It is an excellent idea to have written expectations for communication. These allow each member of the special education team to know in advance what is expected. As one elementary school principal stated, "We have established monthly norms of professional expectations that are communicated, reviewed, and celebrated." For example, for the month of April, the following norms were sent out to every staff member of the principal's school.

Each team member will communicate honestly and respectfully by doing the following:

- Making the effort to express feelings of appreciation, satisfaction, and support
- Discerning whether feelings of dissatisfaction are personal or related to student and family services

- Expressing feelings of dissatisfaction before they become frustrations
- Directing concerns back to the point of origin; presenting concerns with diplomacy and an emphasis on a solution versus personal shortfalls
- Taking advantage of established collaborative meeting times if the issues are program specific
- Talking in private if the issues are personal and being open to the concerns and feelings of others

Clearly, the principal and the school staff have been proactive in their approach to open communication. Open communication is valued as a critical part of a special education process that appropriately and effectively meets student needs. The following two case studies will illustrate these points.

OLIVIA, a paraeducator, worked one on one with Raul throughout his school day. Raul was 10 years old, had cerebral palsy, used a manual wheelchair for mobility, and was included in general physical education. He had the strength and coordination to move his chair independently. Sharon was the physical education teacher for Raul's 3rd-grade class. Before each class, Sharon briefly met with Olivia to discuss her role in supporting Raul during the day's lesson.

For example, the objectives for one day's lesson included locomotor skills (e.g., running, jumping, sliding). This was the first time the class was working on locomotor skills. Since Raul used a wheelchair, Olivia was not sure how he could jump, gallop, or participate in any of the other locomotor skills except running. Sharon explained that when the other students ran, Raul would push his chair fast. When the other students were jumping, Raul would move his chair forward twice and once to the left. For hopping, he would move his chair forward twice and to the left twice. For galloping, he would move his chair backward twice and to the right once. Olivia asked why Raul couldn't just raise one hand to simulate hopping, and Sharon explained that since the rest of the class was working on locomotor skills (moving from point A to point

B), Raul needed to learn to move his chair differently so he could develop the skills needed for wheelchair sport. So, to do movements with his hands was not consistent with his objectives for the lesson. Any modifications needed to be consistent with the objectives of the lesson.

Sharon then handed Olivia an index card with the modifications written on them. Olivia saw that there was no modification for sliding and pointed this out to Sharon. Sharon explained that she did not forget; rather, she wanted Olivia to come up with the modification since she knew Raul best and now understood how to modify the lesson. Together, Olivia and Sharon set up a quality learning experience for Raul.

MICHELE was a middle school aide for a class of students with disabilities. There were 12 students in the class with disabilities ranging from mild to severe. Michele was not assigned to work one on one with a specific student; rather, she supported all of the students as needed. The students received their physical education from Mike, an adapted physical education specialist, who met with the class daily for 40 minutes. Mike planned 2-week units, and he met with Michele at the beginning of each unit to discuss her role in helping the students achieve their goals and objectives.

The upcoming unit was softball. Mike explained to Michele that her role would be to provide specific information about how a student performed a given activity (skill feedback). He explained that his role would be to lead the lesson, instruct the students, and provide skill and behavioral feedback. Mike shared his lesson plans with her, including all of the activities and teaching cues for the skills in the unit. Although this information was helpful, Michele suggested that because she did not know very much about softball, she would have a difficult time knowing whether the students were doing the skills correctly.

Given this honest and important feedback, Mike and Michele planned to meet after school to go over the skills in the softball unit. Mike discussed and demonstrated the progression of each skill and gave Michele a short video to watch on teaching young people to play softball. They decided to meet at lunch the next day so that Mike could answer any questions she might have. They then agreed that Michele would focus on three cues per skill. Mike gave her an index card that had the cues for the skills being taught. Now Michele was better able to assist Mike in observing the students and providing feedback as needed. With both Mike and Michele focused on skill acquisition, they were able to give one-on-one assistance when needed and create a more successful learning environment.

These two scenarios provide real examples of how establishing open communication leads to enhanced learning for students. Open communication also creates an atmosphere of collaboration where each member of the special education team feels valued and appreciated. Through planned collaboration, open communication, and structured meeting times, these teachers and paraeducators have ensured that the needs of students with disabilities are met in the most efficient and effective manner.

In the first example, Sharon and Olivia had already established an open line of communication. Sharon explaining the reasoning behind the modifications allowed Olivia to more actively participate in the lesson and feel more a part of the teaching process. Olivia worked with Raul all day, every day, so she better understood his unique needs and abilities. Because she understood the specific objectives of the lesson, she was able to come up with even better modifications than Sharon. Thus, this example illustrates true collaboration.

In the second example, it is obvious that Mike and Michele had an effective communication and collaboration system. Not only was Michele an active participant in the students' learning, she gained new knowledge in the physical education discipline. Michele felt comfortable asking questions and asking for additional support (i.e., after-school meetings and softball videos). Mike also felt comfortable giving Michele direction and valued her contributions to a positive, effective learning environment. They made a great team and in the end, everyone won—especially the students.

Working to Deflect Conflict Resolution

The earlier examples of Sharon and Olivia and Mike and Michele illustrate efficient, effective special education teams where open communication has

▶ By addressing and solving conflicts early on in the team approach, the paraeducator and the adapted physical education teacher are better able to work as a team with the students and help to create the most ideal environment for learning.

▶ TABLE 3.1 Integral Steps in Conflict Resolution

Key concept	Strategy
Understand the chain of command.	First, you should meet with the teacher to resolve the issue. If meeting with the teacher and using the strategies discussed here fail to bring a resolution, then you should meet with the school principal. If still no resolution can be made, the next step is to meet with the district special education director.
Take an approach of solving the problem together. This will create a mindset for solving the problem objectively and fairly.	Set aside time to meet with the teacher. Start the meeting with the following question: "How can we resolve this issue together?"
Focus on defeating the problem, not each other.	During your meeting with the teacher, if the focus turns on who is right and who is wrong, redirect the meeting to the problem at hand.
Each person's opinion should be valued and discussed.	Take care to listen and respond respectfully to the teacher's opinion. This same courtesy should be afforded to you.
Recognize that there are usually many solutions to one problem.	Try to avoid going into the meeting with the idea that you have already figured out the solution to the problem. Once you suggest a solution, you should then listen to and discuss the teacher's ideas.
Address the conflict early on—don't let it fester and thus create more problems.	Once a problem arises, determine specifically what the problem is and immediately set a time to meet with the teacher. Rarely do problems simply go away, and waiting will typically make the problem worse.

been established. We have discussed several steps that can be taken to create this type of environment. However, there are certain situations that make open communication and collaboration difficult. For example, you and the teacher may disagree on how to best meet a student's needs and have difficulty in coming up with a solution because you both feel strongly about the best course of action to take. In this section, we will discuss conflict resolution and ways to overcome difficult situations. We will also present a case study to illustrate our points.

Difficult situations with others is an ongoing fact of life, but there are a number of techniques that can be used to assist in conflict resolution. Although no one technique works best, it is important to remember a few key concepts (table 3.1).

The special education team approach is all about creating the ideal environment for students to learn and be successful. Addressing and solving conflicts early in their genesis will ensure the stability of the special education team.

When conflicts appear to be highly complex or difficult, it may be helpful to keep in mind Occam's razor. In the 14th century, William of Occam wrote, *"Pluralitas non est ponenda sine necessitate,"* which translates to "Entities should not be multiplied unnecessarily." This is known as *Occam's razor* and is interpreted to mean that often the simplest solution is the best solution. You will find that open communication focusing on the problem itself will often result in a straightforward, simple solution. Let's look at the following illustration.

TAMARA was a first-year paraeducator in a high school. She was assigned to work one on one with Vaughn, who had mental retardation. Vaughn spent most of his school day in a separate class for students with cognitive disabilities. For physical education, Vaughn was included in the general class, where Linda was the general physical education teacher. Linda was beginning the year with a unit on basketball and assumed that Tamara would work directly with Vaughn in order to include him in the lesson. However, Tamara did not know how to assist Vaughn and knew nothing about basketball. Linda began class without meeting with Tamara. Not knowing her role, Tamara sat down and watched. She observed both Vaughn and Linda getting frustrated because Vaughn was having difficulty understanding the directions and completing the tasks. This went on all week. On the following Monday, Tamara got a call from the school principal. At a meeting in his office, he informed Tamara that Linda was upset because Tamara was taking a break when she should be working with Vaughn. Tamara explained that she knew nothing about basketball, was not given any direction on how to assist him, and had no choice but to watch.

In the previous example, Tamara did not feel like she was part of the special education team and Linda had already labeled Tamara as lazy and not wanting to do her job. This type of conflict occurs far too often. Linda should have met with Tamara before the class to clearly explain her expectations for Tamara and to give her direction on how to best include Vaughn. Both Tamara and Linda could have saved themselves the frustration of having the principal mediate and, more importantly, could have added a week of instruction for Vaughn. By recognizing that open communication is critical to a positive, productive learning environment for the students, you will better be able to avoid these situations. If the teacher does not give you direction, then you should approach the teacher and ask. Not everyone is good at communicating and collaborating. Some teachers may not have been trained to appropriately use paraeducators, or they may be so concerned with teaching content that they forget to involve you in the lesson. You can assist those who have difficulty communicating with you by initiating communication and practicing active and reflective listening. Remember, you are a key member of the special education team, and you have the best interests of the student in mind. Without your support, the student may fail.

To begin with, direct, diplomatic communication is the key to resolving conflicts. See table 3.1 for specific examples. If you cannot resolve the conflict with the people involved, then it may be necessary to take additional steps. Figure 3.1 highlights an example of a chain of command to follow for resolving conflicts.

> District Special Education Director
> ↓
> School Principal
> ↓
> Paraeducator ↔ Teacher

▶ **Figure 3.1 Sample chain of command.**

In the rare instance that the two parties involved cannot resolve the problem using the conflict resolution techniques described previously, the problem should be taken to the next level. Typically, this involves the school principal. The principal will act as a mediator in order to define the problem and propose appropriate solutions. If the principal cannot resolve the problem, it should be taken to the next level, typically the school district's special education director. Generally, conflicts can be resolved by the initial parties. Moving to the next level should only occur if you and the teacher cannot resolve the problem through open, direct communication. In the case of Tamara and Linda, Linda should have approached Tamara before going to the principal. She did not realize that Tamara wanted to help but just did not know how. This chain of command is an example and will vary from school to school and from district to district. You should ask your site coordinator for a chain of command in the early weeks of the school session so that if you need help in conflict resolution, you will know the appropriate steps to take.

We have learned in this section that when you establish open communication, all parties benefit—especially the students. Open communication and collaboration reduce conflict and create a fun and positive working environment where all members of the special education team are included and valued. To sum up this section, we have five basic expectations for you.

Expectations of Paraeducators

- Demonstrate constructive interpersonal skills with students and team members.
- Use respectful communication.
- Use open communication.
- Resolve conflicts in timely and appropriate manner.
- Ensure the best possible learning experience for the students.
- The paraeducator is an active, contributing member of the special education team. Open communication and collaboration and the timely and respectful resolution of conflicts can ensure that all members of the team are functioning efficiently. Once this is established, focus on creating a physically and emotionally safe environment for the students.
- Develop a learning community.

Siedentop and Tannehill (2000) have referred to a physically and emotionally safe environment as a *learning community.* In this environment, all learners, including those with significant disabilities, are valued members of the class who are concerned about and contribute to others' growth and well-being. By its very nature, a community of learners celebrates and respects individual differences and attention is paid to the positive attributes that each person brings to the gymnasium. The following list outlines attributes that are representative of students who belong to a learning community (Garcia & Krouscas, 1995; Schaps & Lewis, 1998).

Attributes of Students Who Belong to a Learning Community

1. They take responsibility for their behavior and actions.
2. They support one another.
3. They cooperate with one another.
4. They demonstrate trust for one another.
5. They are committed to the basic values of caring and fairness.

How might you, as a paraeducator, help to establish this type of community? To begin with, it is imperative that you, as well as the physical education teacher, carefully and honestly examine your own potentially harmful attitudes and behaviors toward the students you work with. Do you make gender- or race-stereotyped comments or accept it when others do? Do you interact in a different way based solely on the gender, socioeconomic status, level of motor skillfulness, or race of your students? When intimidation, harassment, or the embarrassment of a student is taking place, do you ignore the behavior? Although this list of questions could continue, the intent is clear: As educators, we must work sensitively and equitably with all students, modeling appropriate behavior (walking the talk) and sensitively intervening when appropriate.

Importance of a Caring Approach to Teaching

In developing a strong community of learners, the demonstration of caring on the part of the teacher and paraeducator is essential. A caring environment is a physical education class (and, hopefully, an entire school) that is committed to treating all students with dignity, protecting them and investing the required time, energy, and expertise to maximize their physical, affective, and intellectual development. Siedentop and Tannehill (2000) have noted that, rather than being a set of tools, caring is a teaching framework within which many positive outcomes can be achieved, both in terms of academic achievement and personal growth. Bosworth (1995) has outlined a number of teaching behaviors that are demonstrated by the caring paraprofessional:

- Being aware of and giving the appropriate amount of assistance to students
- Valuing students as individuals
- Treating students with respect
- Being accepting of others

▶ By ensuring that the students feel cared about and respected, paraeducators help contribute to student learning.

- Making sure that the students understand what is being asked of them
- Carefully checking for understanding
- Designing activities that are fun as well as challenging

Students can identify and, understandably, appreciate paraprofessionals who truly care about their well-being. These professionals clearly enjoy what they're teaching and get involved in their students' lives, both within and outside the gymnasium. These characteristics contrast sharply with those of teachers who have been perceived by students as uncaring. Uncaring professionals are unconcerned about boring tasks, pay little attention to their students' questions and performance, and regularly make disparaging and disrespectful comments, often embarrassing students in front of their peers (Wentzel, 1997). A caring approach leads to personal and social growth and has an extremely positive effect on student learning. According to Goodman, Sutton, and Harkavy (1995), an atmosphere characterized by mutual respect and empathy promotes learning and achievement. It certainly seems logical that when students feel accepted and valued—as opposed to feeling belittled and demeaned—by their peers and teachers, their attention to the task at hand increases.

WHEN Tiffany came into the gym a few minutes early on Monday, she headed over to the bleachers where she usually sat by herself. She was wearing a new Britney Spears T-shirt that Tanya, the paraprofessional, hadn't seen before. Although not a fan of pop music, Tanya talked to Tiffany about the shirt and found out that she'd been to a Britney Spears concert the previous Saturday night and had a great time. Over the course of the 3-minute conversation Tanya found out a little about Tiffany's big passion and, in the bargain, saw her smile for the first time in 2 months.

In the previous story, a small but significant show of interest demonstrated to Tiffany that Tanya cared about her as a person, and it was the beginning of a deeper and more satisfying relationship between the two. Coincidentally, Tiffany gave

physical education more of a try and found that she had a knack for badminton and enjoyed it a lot.

Constructing a Safe Learning Space

Physical education classes are clearly becoming more diverse learning environments. In addition to students from diverse cultures studying together, many students with identifiable disabilities are included in the general education setting. It is important that, beyond examining our own biases, we establish an environment where students can safely share their concerns and questions about classmates who may look or act differently than they're used to. Students must feel free to ask for information about their peers, thereby increasing their understanding and reducing their anxiety. This increased knowledge base will help to improve relationships between students and move the class toward becoming a true community of learners.

As an important contributor to the physical education climate, the paraeducator is able to work toward the establishment of a safe learning space. One way to do this is to be available to talk about potentially difficult issues that are on the minds of your students. Fostering the acceptance and understanding of classmates who are different from the norm can be challenging. Keep the following guidelines in mind when discussing classmates with disabilities in general education classes:

- Listen actively (maintaining eye contact), patiently, and carefully when students speak.
- When it's your turn to speak, do so honestly and openly.
- Listen carefully for truth from each person's perspective.
- Avoid belittling or blaming students.
- Maintain confidentiality at all times.

STEPHEN, a 6th grader in Aaron's class, wanted to feel comfortable with Aaron, but it was hard for him to relax when Aaron came over to him and hugged him. The one time he'd said that he didn't want to be hugged, Aaron pushed him backward—hard. Stephen's policy from then on had been to avoid the new kid who had something called Down syndrome—whatever that was. It wasn't just that he felt nervous around Aaron; it was that he felt badly about the nervousness, like it made him less of a good guy. Stephen thought that it would help to talk to someone about how he felt.

Stephen's feelings in the previous example are certainly common in an inclusive physical education setting. Keeping such feelings bottled up and lacking accurate information about peers with disabilities can only lead to a tense environment characterized by a lack of understanding. The paraeducator skilled in establishing a safe learning space would be sensitive to Stephen's discomfort (by observing his actions and listening to his comments) and be available to listen to and discuss his concerns and give him more accurate information about his classmate.

Summary

Creating an emotionally safe environment for learning requires the establishment and maintenance of communication between the paraeducator and the physical education teacher, resolution of conflicts in a timely and appropriate manner, and acting as a caring professional. The paraeducator is the key to creating an emotionally safe environment where all students are valued members of the class who are concerned for and contribute to others' growth and well-being and where individual differences are celebrated and respected.

CHAPTER 4

Positive Methods for Dealing With Difficult Behavior

Doug Collier

Guiding Questions

▶ How can the learning climate of the gymnasium be improved, thereby reducing the likelihood of behavior problems?

▶ What is positive behavior support (PBS), and what four principles is it based on?

▶ Why should educators avoid punishing students?

▶ Why must educators carefully describe difficult behaviors and understand why they occurred?

▶ What is meant by comprehensive interventions and why are they important to use when dealing with behavior problems?

SIERRA saw that for the third time that week, Carlos was twirling a piece of string he'd found and concentrating on it intently. He wasn't bothering anyone else, but it did look odd and kind of spooked the other 3rd graders. In addition, getting him to pay attention to catching the Frisbee was out of the question. "Should I stop him or let it go?" she asked herself. "It would certainly help if I knew what the physical education teacher and the classroom teacher expect and the right way to deal with this situation." After the physical education class was over, Sierra told the physical education teacher about her uncertainty. The physical education teacher was also unclear about how to deal with Carlos when he became fixated on string and had set up a meeting with his homeroom teacher to discuss the best approach. As it turns out, his homeroom teacher had a simple and effective approach. In the classroom setting, if Carlos began to twirl string, the homeroom teacher would take it from him, telling him calmly and firmly that "he couldn't play with string while he was at school." Carlos accepted this without any problem and got back to the task at hand. Armed with this straightforward and important information, both Sierra (the paraeducator) and the physical education teacher were able to more easily keep Carlos focused on the physical education task at hand. In addition, knowing what was expected of her allowed Sierra to be a lot more comfortable working with Carlos in the physical education setting.

Introduction

Students with developmental disabilities may from time to time (or on a more consistent basis) demonstrate what are commonly referred to as *behavior problems.* As a paraeducator, you are assigned to work with students whose behavior is difficult, and you will find yourself in similar situations that Sierra faced. Clearly, this doesn't make the teaching enterprise easy or enjoyable. Teaching students who struggle with their behavior is often emotionally as well as physically draining and is commonly related to reduced job satisfaction and burnout. From the students' perspective, these difficult behaviors interfere with their learning and the learning of their peers. They often have fewer opportunities to learn new skills and to participate meaningfully in a variety of activities that are available to the general student population (e.g., going out to a restaurant, being a member of a sport team, or bowling at the local alley).

It is important that you are given specific information about the school's approach to behavior management in terms of general philosophy, specific procedures used, and your exact role in dealing with behavior problems. This applies to your own class as well. Are you responsible for specific students with respect to their behavior? If so, are you expected to play a role in developing a behavior plan for a given student, collecting data about the frequency and severity of the given behavior, carrying out the plan, monitoring the plan's effectiveness, or suggesting modifications based on assessment data? Clarifying your role in physical education—as in other educational areas—is vital.

> It is important that you are given specific information about the school's approach to behavior management in terms of general philosophy. Schools may have specific procedures, protocols, exact roles, or behavior contracts when dealing with behavior problems.

Effectively dealing with problematic behavior is probably the most difficult challenge presented to paraeducators and to teachers (Collier & Hebert, 2004), and your employers must give you training that is clear and well thought out—both with regard to best practices in adapted physical education and special education and with regard to the individual students you are responsible for. If you feel inadequately prepared, communicating with your teacher or, if necessary, other support personnel promptly and effectively (using the tools outlined in chapter 3) is imperative. With this preparation and support, working with a student like Carlos from the opening story—and dealing appropriately with his string twirling—will be something you can do well.

Create a Positive Space

Regardless of how many students you are responsible for, there are general considerations that will improve the learning climate of the class and reduce the likelihood of behavior problems.

1. Examine yourself and your beliefs. To effectively deal with difficult behaviors, paraeducators must carefully examine their own philosophies, values, and goals with regard to teaching and learning. For example, you might get frustrated, like this teacher does: "Whenever I go with Alexia to physical education, I just get this tight feeling across my chest. Yes, I know she has been diagnosed with autism—although I'm still not sure what I'm supposed to do with that information. If Alexia is supposed to be ready to be integrated, then she should be able to follow the rules, like everyone else does. We all have things going on. I can't help but feel that she's flapping her hands and looking away just to annoy me when I'm trying my hardest to make it fun."

The following list outlines a number of questions you might ask yourself:

- Do I view part of my role as working to improve my students' behavior? Do I use teaching strategies that will lessen the likelihood that difficult behavior will take place?
- Do I actively seek out information that will help me in effectively teaching students who have problematic behavior?
- Have I thought about which behavior management techniques I find acceptable, and which, for ethical or philosophical reasons, I would not use?
- Have I examined my position regarding where students with challenging behaviors should be educated (e.g., the general education gymnasium or a more segregated setting)?
- Have I examined which behaviors I appreciate as well as behaviors that I find unacceptable? Is my answer different depending on which student I have in mind?

▶ Being positive leads to a productive climate for the students.

Beyond thinking about the questions outlined in the previous list, how do you interact and present yourself during physical education? Are you tuned in to what's going on in the class? Are you aware of potentially disruptive situations and do you stop misbehavior before it starts? How about your enthusiasm? As Lavay, French, and Henderson (2006) point out, your enthusiasm for teaching will be contagious, leading to the positive and nurturing climate we're all striving for.

With regard to Alexia's hand flapping, the paraeducator needs to carefully examine how realistic he's being regarding her following the rules like everyone else. As well, he should carefully examine the reasons for her hand flapping. Although he might be correct—that is, she's flapping her hands and looking away to get a reaction from him—a much more likely reason for the behavior would be that it calms her in stressful situations. The hand flapping may still be a behavior that he may want to consider changing, but it's not one aimed personally at the paraeducator.

2. Catch them being good. It had been a long morning and Maria, the paraeducator, was feeling tired and somewhat irritated as she finished some warm-up tosses with James before the class softball game was to start. All of a sudden, James threw the ball a little too quickly and a little too low. It skipped by Maria and headed toward the fence. She was about to firmly tell him to pay a little more attention and throw with more care when she caught herself. "Hey," she thought, "let's not make a big deal about something that isn't particularly important and probably wasn't done to purposefully bother me." Instead of getting frustrated with James, she jogged after the ball and threw it back to him. He made a nice grab, flashing those major-league hands. Maria commented that she generally saw that kind of catch on television when the Cardinals were playing. James flashed a big grin and threw an off-speed strike right to Maria.

As simple as it sounds, it seems that we pay attention to people when things are not going well. In addition to creating a draining situation by perceiving negativity to be everywhere, students quickly learn that in order to get your attention, the best approach is to act out. The good news, however, is that the opposite is true as well. When we start to pay attention to the good stuff, we begin to see more of it. In this situation, Maria took a deep breath and didn't overreact to James' low and quick throw. Instead, she paid attention to James' good throw in a way that he enjoyed. As a result, things moved on in a positive way for both of them.

A key point here is to pay attention in a way that is motivating and rewarding to the student. Just because lots of students enjoy a high five or a tap on the shoulder, don't assume everyone does. Get to know your students well, and reinforce them in a way that is, indeed, reinforcing.

3. When you ask students to do something, expect them to follow your directions. There are certainly times when you want to give students a choice of activities (e.g., "Frank, would you like to go to the batting station or the fielding station?"), but at other times you expect a specific course of action. If the situation involves a directive, use a calm, pleasant, but firm tone that leaves no doubt that at this time, there isn't a choice involved. Make sure that you give the student adequate time to respond (3 seconds can seem like a long time, but it isn't) and then repeat the directive. If the response you were expecting is not forthcoming, then you can physically, visually, or verbally prompt the student toward the right response. It is imperative that your request

▶ After an appropriate amount of time, a paraeducator can physically prompt and direct the student toward the desired goal.

is reasonable (that is, fair) and that the learner understands what you require.

How to Give a Direct Instruction

1. Use a calm, pleasant, but firm tone.
2. Give the student adequate time to respond.
3. If the student doesn't respond within approximately 3 seconds, prompt the student to respond.
4. Make sure that your request is fair.
5. Make sure that the student understands what you're asking for.

Becoming tense or angry is counterproductive at many levels. Beyond being an unpleasant experience for both you and the student, you could be reinforcing the very behavior that you're trying to remedy. If you tell a student to move over to the blue square and sit quietly and he refuses, your subsequent fit could be just what he's looking for. As noted, stay calm, be firm, wait, and then, if required, prompt him to do what you've requested. If the student doesn't follow through, a more thorough examination of the *why* of his behavior is in order. Understanding his motivation will help you determine a course of action.

4. Does a problem actually exist? It has been suggested that, at least on some occasions, teachers and paraeducators might feel that there is a behavior problem when, in fact, none exists. This could be because of bias on the part of the educator, unreasonable expectations for the student, or an inadequate method to collect objective information. Wolery, Bailey, and Sugai (1988) have outlined several questions to ask if you suspect that there is a problem:

- Is progress being made on instructional objectives?
- Are tasks being completed?
- Is the teacher or paraeducator being relied on excessively?
- Is the behavior interfering with teaching?
- Is there an acceptable level of interaction with other students?
- Is behavior being demonstrated that will not be acceptable in the student's next placement?

If the student is struggling with one or more of these issues, there might be a problem situation. At this point, the important question once again is to ask yourself *why* the student is struggling physically, intellectually, socially, or behaviorally. Only through understanding what motivates a student can you thoughtfully and positively address the problem.

Skill-Building Approach to Dealing With Challenging Behavior

Over the past 15 years there has been a profound movement away from punishing and coercing people in order to change their behavior (that is, attempting to control their behavior through the threat of or escape from unpleasant events) toward a much more positive, affirming, and ethical approach to behavior change. Referred to as *positive behavior support* (PBS) (Safran & Oswald,

2003), this approach is based on the following four principles:

1. An understanding that people (including paraeducators) should not control students but try to support them as they work on changing their behavior

2. A strongly held belief that there are reasons behind even the most difficult behaviors and that people should be treated with respect and compassion at all times

3. The application of a growing body of knowledge about how to better understand people and make humane changes in their lives (both in terms of their environment and their skills) that ultimately lead to more appropriate behavior

4. A conviction that it is important to move away from coercive and controlling approaches to behavior management

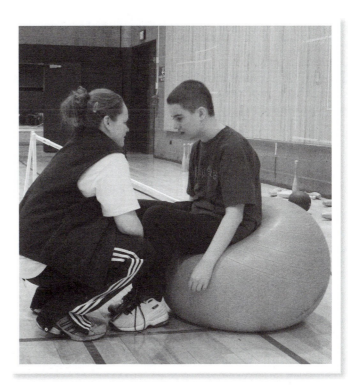

▶ Paraeducators should support students with disabilities as the students work on changing their behavior.

As you can see, PBS moves dramatically away from a reactive, punishing approach that is often ineffective and more for the teachers' and paraeducators' short-term well-being than for the benefit of the student. Although ethically questionable and often ineffective, professionals still select negative approaches, such as verbal reprimands, time-outs, movement to a more restrictive physical education setting, and corporal punishment. These approaches may give immediate relief from a difficult situation, but they are rarely effective in reducing or eliminating problematic behavior. As well as not working, these punitive approaches are time consuming and emotionally draining for both the paraprofessional and the student. Sugai and Horner (2001) and Gable, Quinn, Rutherford, Howell, and Hoffman (2000) have outlined specific reasons to avoid punishment.

Practical and Ethical Reasons to Avoid Punishment

1. Punishment leads to environments that control students rather than support them.

2. Punishment sets the stage for and reinforces antisocial behavior.

3. Punishment shifts accountability away from the paraeducator and school.

4. Punishment leads to a more adversarial relationship between the student and the paraeducator.

5. Punishment may reinforce the inappropriate behavior, thus making it worse.

6. Punishment doesn't teach alternative, effective options to the inappropriate behavior.

7. Punishment does not address the reason for the behavior.

8. Punishment may result in injury.

9. Punishment may result in the student avoiding the environment (i.e., the gymnasium becomes a punishing place to be).

10. Punishment may result in unanticipated and unwanted side effects.

PBS focuses on both setting up environments that prevent problematic behavior and teaching meaningful and useful skills that are effective alternatives to the problematic behavior. In addition to attempting to reduce problematic behavior through the reinforcement of desired behavior and the ignoring or punishing of unwanted behavior, PBS includes a wide range of individualized strategies that result in "important social and learning outcomes while preventing problem behavior" (Turnbull et al., 2002, p. 377). PBS takes place in natural environments (such as the gymnasium or an after-school swim program) where paraeducators, teachers, recreational specialists, and families can successfully implement the support strategies. This team-oriented approach supports people with challenging behaviors within all their daily activities across many different environments.

PBS includes a wide range of individualized strategies such as:

TEACHING DESIRABLE BEHAVIORS— SOME IMPORTANT CONSIDERATIONS

1. Clarify your expectations
2. Make your expectations realistic
3. Teach effective alternative behaviors
4. Teach behaviors that are valued and reinforced by other people
5. Remember to "fade" the supports needed for desirable behavior
6. Teach effective and acceptable alternative means of communication
7. Establish consistent routines

As mentioned, teaching more appropriate and equally effective ways of responding along with retooling the environment has resulted in significant reductions in problem behavior, important educational gains, and improved quality of life. In a nutshell, we are thinking less about fixing a student who is struggling and more about what we ourselves are currently doing and what we can change in order to increase the student's quality of life.

Important Elements of Positive Behavioral Support Plans

PBS plans should begin by outlining what is known about the problem situation, or what is happening and why. This part of the PBS plan has four parts:

- Examining positive contributions
- Carefully describing the target behaviors
- Finding problem routines
- Conducting a functional behavioral assessment

> Important elements of PBS plans include doing the following:
>
> • Examining positive contributions
> • Carefully describing the target behaviors
> • Finding problem routines
> • Conducting a functional behavioral assessment
> • Using comprehensive interventions

Examine Positive Contributions

WHEN the physical education class visited the cardiovascular center to work on their individualized fitness plans, Steve, an 11th-grade student with Down syndrome, not only completed the circuit independently, he was a great help to his buddy Justin, a typically developing student who struggled with his form, while performing the free weight exercises. Steve, having excellent skills with regard to weight training, did the circuit with Justin, helping him maintain proper posture and breathing. This was a tremendous help to both Justin and the physical education teacher (who was able to spend time with other students who needed his help and more carefully monitor the weight room for safety purposes). As well, it was evident to Steve's classmates that irrespective of his disability, he was a tremendously competent weight trainer.

The first step in setting up PBS plans is considering the strengths and interests of the student. This is extremely important since successful plans are built on these positive contributions. Examining and using a student's strengths sets a more positive tone to a sometimes difficult undertaking and starts the paraprofessional working on the support plan (e.g., helping with the design, carrying out the plan, or both) and thinking about potential solutions (e.g., preferred activities, strengths, positive reinforcers). With respect to the previous example, Steve's interest in and willingness to help his classmates is clearly a positive attribute that can be built on.

Describe the Target Behaviors

TYRONE, a general physical educator, was frustrated with Suzanne's behavior. "I certainly get the message that Suzanne doesn't enjoy archery," he thought, "but her angry behavior just makes her paraeducator, as well as the other students, nervous and makes me question whether she should be in regular physical education at all. Maybe students with autism should be in adapted physical education classes with other students who have autism. Her outbursts are hard for me, the paraeducator, and the other students to understand and to handle. I think it's only a matter of time before I get calls from parents worried about their children's safety."

It is critical that all people working with the student (including the paraeducator who, as discussed, often has the primary responsibility of carrying out behavior plans) understand whether a targeted behavior has taken place. Going back to the previous example, exactly what was Suzanne's troublesome behavior? Although it may seem obvious, even experienced teachers disagree about whether or not a behavior has taken place and the reason for the observed behavior. When staff members (e.g., paraeducators, peer tutors, general education teachers, physical education teachers) are working as a team, this problem is compounded. Common errors when attempting to accurately describe behaviors include describing a single behavior as problematic when in fact there are multiple problems, describing behaviors in very general terms (e.g., Suzanne is antisocial; Peter is mean-spirited; Suzanne is angry), and basing the description on a given diagnostic category or disability (e.g., autism, Asperger's syndrome) instead of observable events (e.g., scratches another student, runs away).

Especially when more than one person is working with a student (as is generally the case), it is important that everyone can recognize, without question, a specific behavior. If Jane is antisocial, does that mean she prefers to catch and throw a ball by herself in a distant corner of the gym, or does it mean that when another student asks her to play catch, Jane screams and scratches? What is antisocial behavior to one person may not be antisocial behavior to another. "Jane acts in an antisocial fashion during physical education" would not pass our ambiguity test. "Jane scratches other children" would.

A clear and thorough description gives us information about how often the behavior has taken place (frequency), where it happened (locus), what it looked like (topography), how long it happened for (duration), how strong it was (intensity), and how long it took to occur (latency). A clear description of the target behavior has the added benefit of placing the emphasis on how to help the student with the behavior as opposed to blaming the student.

Find Problem Routines

IT was an awesome class! Candice could jump rope better than anyone else in the 5th-grade class, and the routine she did impressed all the students. For 5 minutes she wasn't the girl with attention deficit/hyperactivity disorder (ADHD). She was just Candice, a great rope jumper. And then class was over and the students lined up to get a drink of water. There was one drinking fountain with 16 children waiting. Candice was 12th in line. All of a sudden, the waiting—with students very close to each other—became too much. She grabbed her own wrist and bit hard.

A vital part of PBS is to identify the context—that is, the where or when—of problematic behaviors. Referred to as *routines* (Horner, 2000), these situations might involve a particular class (e.g., art, physical education), activity (e.g., using a parachute to work on upper-body strength and teamwork), or transition (e.g., moving from the swimming pool to the locker room, waiting in line for a drink of water at the fountain). By taking a thorough look at the student's daily schedule, we can often pinpoint times and places where problematic behavior is more likely to occur. Equally important, we are able to identify times and places where problematic behavior *doesn't* occur. Both types of information are important in developing an effective PBS plan. Features of the environments where problematic behavior is unlikely to take place can be identified and built into strategies to improve behavior in other environments. If problematic behaviors occur frequently in specific environments, characteristics of these environments can be identified and modified. For example, Peter loved to bowl, but he had a difficult time concentrating because the electronic scoring system that was projected on the ceiling fascinated him. When the manager disconnected the electronic system, Peter got back to bowling.

In the case of Candice's wrist biting in the previous story, it's unfortunate that the educators in charge of the class put her in a position to fail. They should have realized that Candice didn't have the skills to stand in line for the amount of time required. Instead of having her wait in line, Candice could have walked with a paraeducator to an unused fountain down the hall.

Conduct a Functional Behavioral Assessment

AT the beginning of class, the students generally got into four-person squads for 3 minutes. When he was told to do this, Ryan would scream and hit his chin with his fist. Sarah, the general physical educator, was consistent in how she dealt with the situation. She firmly told him to stop hitting. She then repeated the command to get into his squad. If Ryan continued to scream and hit himself (which he generally did), she calmly but firmly moved him to the quiet square to think about how he behaved. Almost immediately, he calmed down and she then let him take part in the physical education activity. At that point, they'd moved from the squads into the first game.

A functional behavioral assessment (FBA) looks beyond the behavior itself and asks *why* somebody behaves in a particular fashion. What are the events that reliably set the stage for (predict) and follow (maintain) problem behaviors? If we don't have a good understanding of why someone is doing something, the approach we take to improve the situation is just a guess. In the previous example, Ryan had probably found out that screaming and hitting himself were effective in getting him out of a situation that was extremely upsetting for him (being in a squad with three other students). The physical education teacher had been rewarding Ryan's screaming and self-abusive behavior without knowing it. When Ryan screamed, he was allowed to leave his four-person squad—exactly what he wanted.

Although students with disabilities sometimes show extremely challenging behaviors, these should not be thought of as willful or malicious. Rather, the behaviors are connected to the student's disability and represent an effort to exert some control over the environment, although in a fashion that is problematic (to the student and often to other students and the teacher as well) and limiting. Gable et al. (2000) have suggested that FBAs focus on the function of the given behavior (that is, what the person is trying to accomplish). Functions of behavior can be divided into five general categories:

1. The function is to *get* something:
   - Social reinforcement (e.g., a thumbs-up for making a nice pass)
   - Tangible reinforcement (e.g., a smiley-face sticker)
2. The function is to *escape or avoid* something:
   - An unpleasant task (e.g., a difficult movement task requiring skills not in the student's repertoire)
   - An unpleasant situation (e.g., rolling a ball back and forth with an unpleasant peer)
3. The function is *both* (e.g., to escape a difficult skill task and to get access to a corner of the gym where there is an intriguing mechanical device).
4. The function is to *access sensory stimulation* (visual, auditory, tactile, or gustatory) (e.g., waving hands back and forth in front of the face to get an interesting light effect).
5. The function is to *communicate* something (e.g., "This gymnasium is too loud and chaotic, and I want to leave").

What is the function of the behavior?

- The function is to *get* something.
- The function is to *escape or avoid*.
- The function is *both* to escape a difficult situation and to get something of value.
- The function is to *access sensory stimulation.*
- The function is to *communicate* something.

Conducting an FBA might be extremely simple or complex. Regardless, an FBA that is thought through and administered well will result in (a) identification of persons, places, and events that reliably predict where problematic behaviors are most and least likely to take place; (b) identification of the consequences that are thought to maintain the problematic behavior; (c) a tentative hypothesis regarding what is causing the behaviors; and (d) some type of observations that support the tentative hypothesis (Horner, 2000).

In the example at the beginning of this section, discussion with Ryan's classroom teacher and parents showed that when he had to sit within a couple of feet of another student for more than 20 seconds or so, he became extremely agitated regardless of the setting. From then on, when it was time to get into squads, Ryan was allowed to sit a little farther away from his mates. He sat quietly, attended well, and stopped screaming and hitting himself. The tentative hypothesis was that sitting close to people bothered Ryan, making him agitated in physical education. Based on a little research, his educators chose to let him sit farther away and the results were positive. The solution isn't always as simple as this, but it often is.

Using Comprehensive Interventions

PBS includes comprehensive intervention as well as the careful assessment of difficult behaviors as outlined in the previous section.

A PBS plan is comprehensive when *all* problematic behaviors are addressed, it is based on a functional assessment, it is applied throughout the day, and it incorporates multiple interventions (e.g., instruction, environmental changes, consequences for behavior). Because a single intervention or procedure is rarely effective in producing durable and generalizable results, parents and practitioners are looking for procedures that are effective in combination. Three areas that have received considerable attention are curricular revision, student choice, and functional communication training.

A PBS plan is comprehensive when *all* problematic behaviors are addressed, it is based on a functional assessment, it is applied throughout the day, and it incorporates multiple interventions.

Curricular Revision

MEGHAN had joined the middle school at midterm from a similarly sized school in southern Oregon. Yung, the physical educator, hadn't ever worked with a student diagnosed with Down syndrome, but he wanted to teach functional, age-appropriate leisure skills that she could use recreationally and were enjoyable. In speaking to her mom and dad, he found out that she liked softball a lot and had some good fundamental skills. It was a total shock to him that her behavior was problematic whenever they took ground balls. Meghan would put her hands on her hips and defiantly refuse to participate. Meghan's mom came to watch class one day and noted that, although her daughter was a capable fielder, she preferred to play on the right side of the infield (first or second base) as opposed to the left side (third base or shortstop), where Yung had been positioning her. She went on to explain that Meghan felt very insecure about throwing the ball across the infield and that this insecurity had led to inappropriate behaviors in the past. Yung moved her to the right side, where she did very well.

If the functional assessment suggests that problematic behavior is maintained by avoiding specific tasks, these tasks should be carefully analyzed to identify the features that are punishing to the student (e.g., clarity of instruction, length of the task). The intention is not to remove difficult tasks and replace them with simple ones. Rather, the goals of the program should be maintained, with greater attention paid to details of the task that may be punishing for the learner. For example, the class may be playing a game of tag, which involves running and dodging. Although this activity may be appropriate for all students, a student with an identifiable disability may have a difficult time handling the noise and constant movement and changes of direction. Given that the skills involved are meaningful for the student, a modification might involve playing multiple games of tag with fewer students and thus less noise and unexpected movement.

Student Choice

Strong evidence suggests that when a student is given choices, behavior problems are reduced (Dyer, Dunlap, & Winterling, 1990). Two reasons have been suggested for this. First, when presented with a choice, students with disabilities will pick the least punishing option, thus reducing the likelihood that the challenges presented will result in problematic behavior. On a positive note, this choice will lead to more reinforcing situations and thus to greater rewards for the student. Second, Dunlap and colleagues (1994) have suggested that if the student chooses an activity, fewer behavior problems take place than when the same activity is chosen by the teacher. This is thought to happen because when a student actively chooses to do something, the punishing aspects of tasks are reduced. The message regarding choice is not that students with behavior problems should at all times decide what they can and cannot do but that the inclusion of options in their daily schedule may reduce challenging behaviors.

Students should be taught how to make choices if they don't appear to have this skill. This can be done by offering two or more clear options to students and then reinforcing students appropriately when they make a choice. For example, it is time to play some badminton and you know that Dante, your partner, isn't particularly excited about this activity. The two of you walk over to the badminton court. When you both get there, he is clearly given the choice of using the black plastic racket or the green aluminum racket. When he chooses, you let him know in a positive and supportive fashion that he's chosen wisely. It's then time for you and Dante to have a good rally.

Functional Communication Training

IT was amazing. Luz used to dread her 6th hour physical education class. At some point in the lesson, something, she was never sure what, would set Anthony off and he would suddenly let out a piercing yell. Needless to say, she wasn't the only one on edge. His classmates seemed nervous most of the time and weren't particularly fond of being his partner or working at a station with him. Luz is still not always sure what will upset Anthony, but by teaching him to approach her and pull on her sleeve when things are upsetting him, she's been able to give him breaks when he needs them, without the screaming. In fact, the screaming has stopped entirely. At the same time, Luz has been getting better at setting up movement tasks that interest Anthony and pairing him with peers that understand him. If she blows it, though, he has the tools to let her know in a way that works for her, the class, and him.

Although placed third on this brief list, functional communication training has been proposed as a proactive, skill-building approach to both improving quality of life and combating difficult behaviors. Many practitioners and researchers feel strongly that communication is important with regard to the appearance and maintenance of difficult behaviors. Functional communication training involves teaching students ways of responding that are socially appropriate, produce the same result (acquiring preferred activities or objects or escaping aversive environments), and are more effective than the problematic behavior—that is, they require less effort, repetitions, or time to achieve the same ends.

▶ Finding a form of functional training communication that works for the student and the paraeducator is a proactive way to enable the student to feel comfortable with indicating vital issues to the paraeducator.

Considerations When Implementing a PBS Plan

Paraeducators, physical educators, adapted physical educators, and recreation specialists may be excited about recent findings that hold great hope for reducing the extremely challenging behaviors often present with individuals who have disabilities, but to be effective, PBS must be doable. In other words, beyond being attractive in theory, we must be able to carry out this approach in our day-to-day interactions with children. There are a number of serious concerns that must be addressed in order to effectively implement PBS strategies.

To begin with, PBS will not work if the effects of the intervention on the other children are negative (i.e., their education is compromised). Similarly, if paraeducators, physical education teachers, and other staff members feel that the requirements of the interventions are overwhelming and don't let them get on with the business of teaching, the plan won't work. To be effective, PBS has to

1. be consistent with the skills and values of the people doing the implementation,
2. have adequate resources to back it up, and
3. have administrative support.

As you think about your own experience, it should become clear that approaches that are uncomfortable for you and the people you work with will probably not be implemented. If they are, the implementation will likely be inconsistent and, therefore, ineffective. If someone working with a student doesn't have the ability to carry out a procedure or the comfort level with the procedure is low (i.e., the procedure is thought to be embarrassing or dehumanizing to the individual or unfair to the other students), another approach should be considered. Similarly, you must have enough time to carry out the procedure, adequate equipment, and support from your supervisors. Support should include, but is certainly not limited to, the opportunity to develop effective teaching and behavior management tools for students with challenging behaviors. These opportunities may include workshops; in-service training sessions; one-to-one discussions with other professionals; and videotape, audiotape, or written training materials.

Summary

Teaching students with extremely challenging behaviors is, of course, extremely challenging in its own right. By approaching problems in a positive, respectful, systematic, and comprehensive fashion, we increase the likelihood that students with disabilities will have many opportunities to actively and meaningfully take part in their classes and communities.

CHAPTER 5

Instruction Strategies

Sherry L. Folsom-Meek and Rocco Aiello

Guiding Questions

▶ How is the paraeducator involved in each of the four levels of support?

▶ Name one modification of the environment, equipment, or rules that you might use with your students in physical education class.

▶ What is prompting and how is it related to fading?

▶ What is positive reinforcement and how is it related to fading?

▶ Which teaching style might be used with a learner you are working with now?

▶ Describe how paraeducators can work with physical education teachers and peer tutors.

LARS, a student with severe mental retardation, was in the 10th grade. His IEP stated that he was to receive some of his physical education instruction with his peers, with support from Mrs. Anderson, the paraeducator, who spent most of her day with Lars. One month Lars' physical education class had a bowling unit. Lars was excited about it because he had been bowling with his family and really enjoyed it; therefore, the IEP team decided that Lars could function in a general physical education class for the bowling unit. Mr. Davis, Lars' physical education teacher, was not very creative at adapting activities to meet students' needs, and he told Mrs. Anderson, "Help Lars because I don't have time to work with him." He gave Mrs. Anderson no guidance on what to do. Fortunately, Mrs. Anderson had received some training the previous year from the district's adapted physical education teachers. Because of Mr. Davis' lack of helpfulness, Mrs. Anderson called the bowling center to ask them if they had bumper guards. They did, and Mrs. Anderson arranged for them to be installed in the farthest lane from the entryway before Lars' bowling class.

On the first day of the unit, the class, Mrs. Anderson, and Mr. Davis arrived at the bowling center. Mrs. Anderson assisted Lars in paying his money, finding the correct shoes, and picking out an appropriate bowling ball. Lars needed no assistance in putting on his shoes, but he did need a reminder as to which shoe should go on which foot. Mrs. Anderson had arranged for Lars to bowl with a group of three of his peers. She told Lars to watch his peers bowl and cued him when it was his turn. The first time she used physical guidance to help him deliver the bowling ball. Fortunately the scoring was done automatically. Lars was thrilled when he saw colored lights on the scoreboard, and he understood that he scored some points. Mrs. Anderson continued to remind Lars to watch his peers bowl, but she no longer needed to give him physical guidance. The bumper guards were eventually put away.

On the last day of the bowling unit, Lars was able to go to the counter to pay his money and select his shoes. He asked one of his peers to help him select a bowling ball. He sat down out of the way to put on his shoes, and Mrs. Anderson tied them for him. Lars joined his peer group and watched them bowl while waiting for

his turn. Lars' bowling skills greatly improved during the unit, and a lot of high fives were given among the learners in Lars' group. At the end of class, Lars removed his bowling shoes, put on his school shoes, and took his bowling shoes to the counter. He then put his bowling ball away and joined his peers in leaving the bowling center, with Mrs. Anderson following them at a short distance.

Introduction

The previous story illustrates several situations that may occur in physical education for students with disabilities. The purpose of this chapter is to present instructional strategies for working with learners with disabilities in such situations. Paraeducators who spend their days with one or more students with disabilities are perhaps in the best position to aid these learners because they have already developed rapport with them, know them, and know behavior management techniques that tend to work with them. You, the paraeducator, are a highly valued member of learners' IEP teams. This chapter should aid in your understanding of common instructional strategies in the physical education setting. The following topics are covered: levels of support, adaptations and modifications, teaching strategies, and peer tutoring.

Levels of Support

Paraeducators provide a variety of support services for learners with disabilities. Both the teacher's and your knowledge of support needed by each student dictates what you will be asked to do in the physical education classroom. A number of support services are needed in physical education, and Sherrill (2004) classifies these levels on a continuum by intensity, from least to most support. The four levels, their description, and an example of the paraeducator's role with each level are given in table 5.1.

Paraeducators use all four levels of support with students with disabilities in varied physical education tasks. Ultimately the goal is for you to assist learners by providing lesser amounts of support over time. This should allow them to become more independent. For example, a learner might move from extensive to limited support during a bowling

TABLE 5.1 Levels of Support and Paraeducator's Role

Level of support	Description of level	Example of paraeducator's role
Intermittent	• Needed part of the time (short term). • Usually prearranged.	Paraeducator is available to come to physical education class.
Limited	• Planned ahead of time for paraeducator to come to class to assist learner. • Paraeducator needed during some units but not all.	Paraeducator assists learner in swimming unit but not in badminton unit.
Extensive	• Occurs in most activities. • Paraeducator works with learner most of the time in physical education class.	Paraeducator provides assistance to learner during many activities or games.
Pervasive	• Needed constantly. • Paraeducator works with learner during all of the physical education class.	Paraeducator works with the same learner throughout the school day, including physical education class.

Based on C. Sherrill, 2004, *Adapted physical activity, recreation, and sport: Crossdisciplinary and lifespan* (Boston: McGraw-Hill).

unit, as Lars did in the opening story. Over time, the learner may learn how to go to the counter to get bowling shoes, and your support would not be necessary for this task. However, it may still be necessary for you to help with other tasks, such as choosing a bowling ball.

Adaptations and Modifications

The term *adaptation* means "assessing and managing variables and services so as to meet unique needs and achieve desired outcomes" (Sherrill, 2004, p. 7). The term *modification* has a similar meaning. Adaptations and modifications are commonly made in physical education classes. According to Sherrill (2004, p. 10), "All good physical education is adapted physical education," meaning that adaptations and modifications are constantly made to meet the needs of all learners in any given physical education class. Master physical education teachers demonstrate the ability to make adaptations and modifications on the spot as needed. Examples of adaptations and modifications are shown in table 5.2.

TABLE 5.2 Sample Modifications

Environment	Equipment	Rules
Cones or dots to indicate boundaries and station area	Oversized rackets in badminton	Four hits rather than three in volleyball
Cones or dots to establish or maintain routines	Trainer rather than regulation volleyballs	Nine players instead of six in volleyball
Ramps for delivering bowling ball	Brightly colored balls	Batting tee in softball
Footies or other markers to indicate foot placement in throwing	Large balls	Tennis balls bounce twice
Ground surfaces appropriate for all learners in class	Fat and short plastic bats	Runner gets to first base before being tagged
Gymnastic mats in pool for horizontal support	Balls of different textures	Serve closer to the net in net sports
	Softer balls	
	Balls with tails	

See PE Central's Web site (www.pecentral.org) and *Strategies for Inclusion* (Lieberman & Houston-Wilson, 2002) for a more extensive list of adaptations.

Criteria can also be modified to fit the needs of the learner. Criteria are performance standards associated with behavioral objectives. For example, you may be counting the number of trials a learner performs a skill correctly and recording results on a checklist. A common criterion for skill learning is 80%, 4 out of 5 trials, or 8 out of 10 trials. For learners who need more practice to learn the skill, a criterion of 8 out of 10 trials is more appropriate than a smaller number of trials. These are the criteria commonly used with learners with moderate to severe disabilities. Learners with severe disabilities need even more structured criteria, such as 10 consecutive trials correct (Dunn, Morehouse, & Fredericks, 1986). Whenever criteria are not met, the trial process must begin again at square one. If learners are having difficulty, the task may be adapted on the spot to be more achievable (e.g., throwing the ball from a shorter distance, catching a lighter ball, kicking a stationary ball instead of a moving ball).

ONE objective Joey had been working on was throwing a Wiffle ball overhand a distance of one-quarter of a gym length four out of five times. Mrs. Johnson, the paraeducator, gave Joey verbal cues and recorded the number of times he threw the ball the required distance. He succeeded in throwing the ball the correct distance in three out of five trials. Because Joey didn't meet the criterion of four out of five times, he went back to square one. When Mrs. Johnson started the trial process again, Joey threw the ball the designated distance four times in a row. Joey had achieved the objective and was ready to move on to a more difficult objective.

Teaching Strategies

There are a number of facets to teaching physical education. First, the learning environment must be safe. Second, all students need to be challenged. Third, tasks need to be communicated to the learners. Because of the important role of paraeducators, they must be familiar with various techniques so they can effectively assist physical educators. Effective teachers and paraprofessionals are able to juggle these three facets.

Learners need to be taught rules, routines, and expectations in physical education class. Classroom rules should be taught, listed, and posted. Consequences for breaking rules need to be clear to learners. Both physical education teachers and paraeducators must be consistent in enforcing these rules. Students not only need to be taught routines but also need to practice them. Some common routines include entering the physical education classroom, responding to an attention signal, waiting for directions, listening when the teacher is talking, attending to starting and stopping signals, dressing in physical education attire, and closing the class. Some examples of routines that might be established in physical education class

▶ Paraeducators will always be working on modifying and adapting physical education class to help meet the needs of all the students. An example of this is using a tot dock, which allows learners to sit or stand up on it when they are unable to touch the bottom of the pool.

are students hugging the ball (holding the ball close to themselves) until everyone has one, use of the word *freeze* for the stopping signal, and throwing or tossing the ball or beanbag into a container when finished with it (Folsom-Meek, 1991).

Although expectations should be clear from classroom rules and performance objectives, they need to be taught to the students as well. Your role in rules, routines, and expectations is to assist the physical education teacher. For example, when Lars went to the bowling center with his class, the routines at the beginning of class were paying the money, finding shoes that were the correct size, and picking out a bowling ball.

Auxter, Pyfer, and Huettig (2005) have identified some teaching strategies for adapted physical education. First, use positive behavior management techniques. Second, ask learners to repeat directions before beginning the activity. Third, use task analyses and reinforce each step of the task. The data-based gymnasium (Dunn et al., 1986) program for learners with severe disabilities is based on a one-on-one relationship between the teacher or paraeducator and learner. This program has a number of units containing task analyses of skills. Each task analysis contains a terminal behavioral objective written in behavioral terms (observable and measurable), prerequisite skills, and phases and steps in learning the skill. In addition, each Special Olympics sport skill manual contains a behavioral objective and task analyses for the objective. Physical education teachers should furnish the task analyses for you to use. Table 5.3 is an example of a task analysis for roller-skating. Note that each phase is a meaningful activity by itself.

The teacher and paraeducator can adapt the environment to meet all learners' needs. For the most part, the environment should be the same each class period if at all possible. For example, where and how the equipment is placed is

▶ **TABLE 5.3   Task Analysis for Roller-Skating**

Terminal objective	Student roller-skates to a point 30 feet (9 meters) away, turns around, returns to designated spot, and stops.
Prerequisite skills	Recognize right and left, put on skates, lace skates, and tie skates.
Phase I	The student shuffles stocking feet across the floor in a skating fashion.
Phase II	The student wears a carpet square on one foot and slides the foot along the floor.
Phase III	The student wears a carpet square on each foot and slides across the floor in a skating fashion.
Phase IV	The student puts one skate on and pushes self along the floor on the carpet.
Phase V	The student repeats the last phase with the skate on the other foot.
Phase VI	The student uses some support device while moving along the carpet on two skates (chair, walker, helper, banister, big box with the bottom cut out).
Phase VII	The student skates on the floor using the same form of support as listed in phase VI.
Phase VIII	The student skates on the floor with the assistance of a teacher.
Phase IX	The student skates using the proper skating style and stops when appropriate.
Phase X	The student roller-skates to a point 30 feet (9 meters) away, turns, and returns to the designated spot and stops.
The following steps apply to phases VI-X	10 feet (3 meters) 15 feet (4.5 meters) 20 feet (6 meters) 25 feet (7.5 meters)

Adapted from J.M. Dunn, J.W. Morehouse, and H.D.B. Fredericks, 1986, *Physical education for the severely handicapped: A systematic approach to a data based gymnasium* (Austin, TX: Pro-Ed), 155. By permission of John M. Dunn, Southern Illinois University Carbondale.

important. It should be in the same area for each class. Although lesson content will vary, the order of events should be predictable. The environment can be made smaller or larger when necessary. Some experts (Schultheis, Boswell, & Decker, 2000) have suggested making the space smaller for learners with autism by using gymnastic mats to mark off learning stations, thereby helping them concentrate on the task at hand rather than extraneous stimuli.

Choice of teaching strategies is highly dependent on a number of variables. Whatever the age of the student, activity choices need to be meaningful and developmentally appropriate. It is inappropriate for learners with cognitive disabilities to be given activities based on their mental age alone (i.e., it is inappropriate for older learners with mental retardation to play the child's game of Duck, Duck, Goose or other games for young children). Typically, the focus of physical education is for younger learners to learn a variety of basic movement skills and for older learners to learn lifelong physical activities they will use in the community (Auxter et al., 2005; Special Olympics, 1989). Physical education is not about zero-sum games (one winner and one loser) and elimination games. It is about maximum participation, learning new skills with success, and cooperation.

Another important teaching technique is classroom management. Special education teachers, paraeducators, and adapted physical education teachers typically use similar behavior management techniques. These techniques are often based on learning theory. Some of these techniques include prompting, feedback (reinforcement), and fading.

Prompting

Prompting is a term that refers to giving brief signals or instructions (cues) that tell the learner what to do. These signals should be the same each time and should not be repeated until the learner makes a response (Dunn et al., 1986; Sherrill, 2004). Prompting may be verbal (V), modeling (M) or demonstration, and physical guidance (P). Prompts can also be environmental, where the stimulus is presented to the learners and they respond independently (I) (e.g., giving a student a ball to kick or placing a rack of basketballs inside the gymnasium door and teaching students to take one when they enter the gym). The abbreviations (V, M, P, and I) can be used in recording data from students' performance.

Seaman, DePauw, Morton, and Omoto (2003) have devised a prompting hierarchy from least to most extensive prompts. This hierarchy is listed in table 5.4.

▶ **TABLE 5.4 Prompting Hierarchy**	
Prompt	**Example**
Natural cue	Jose picks up a basketball from the ball cart when he enters the gym.
Gestural cue	Ms. Jones, the paraeducator, shakes her head to signal "no" when Jose starts to move away from the group.
Indirect verbal prompt	Jose is touching other students when Ms. Jones is giving directions. Ms. Jones says, "Jose, what do you need to do?"
Modeling	Jose watches his peers deliver the bowling ball.
Symbolic prompt (pictorial or written)	Jose, who has autism, learns best when presented with pictures showing him what he is to do.
Direct verbal prompt	Ms. Jones tells Jose to throw the ball overhead as far as he can.
Minimal physical prompt	Ms. Jones barely touches Jose's leg to indicate that it is the foot to step onto.
Partial physical prompt	Ms. Jones touches Jose's leg and begins to move it.
Full physical prompt	Ms. Jones guides Jose through a forward roll.

Adapted, by permission, from J.A. Seaman et al., 2007, *Making connections: From theory to practice in adapted physical education* (Scottsdale, AZ: Holcomb Hathaway), 228.

▶ After trying other types of prompting, paraeducators can use physical guidance to achieve the desired goals from the students.

Verbal prompts are used the most often and are frequently paired with modeling (demonstration). When modeling for learning skills is used, care must be taken that skills are performed correctly. Physical guidance should be used only when the other types of prompts do not work. However, learners with more severe disabilities may require a great deal of physical prompting, at least in the beginning stages. In the opening story, Mrs. Anderson used physical guidance the first time to assist Lars in bowling. After that, she instructed him to watch his peers (modeling). The ultimate goal is to have learners prompt themselves independently when appropriate. However, there may be situations in which the more basic prompts are necessary for safety or classroom management reasons.

Feedback

Feedback, or reinforcement, is an essential component of learning. It should be specific to the task rather than to the learner. For example, you might say "Nice running" or "Good try" rather than "Good boy" or "Good girl." You should wait to deliver feedback until the learner is finished with the task. Two common types of feedback are positive and corrective.

Positive reinforcement (praise) is more effective than criticism and can be used when a student performs a task, shows effort, and follows directions. Examples of positive feedback are "Nice job of bending your knees" or "I loved the way you watched the ball." An example of how young learners can reinforce themselves is when the teacher or paraeducator tells preschool children to hug themselves for reinforcement. You can also have learners clap their hands for themselves. Still another method of positive reinforcement is when learners reinforce each other by clapping and cheering for peers. In our story, the group of four bowlers and Mrs. Anderson cheered each other on and gave lots of high fives.

Shaping is a term that refers to reinforcing learners for performance that indicates progress but is not at the criterion level of the objective. With shaping, successive approximations (steps toward reaching the objective) are reinforced. Learners should be reinforced for their performance in each phase.

Corrective feedback gives students information about how they performed the task so they will perform the task more effectively. An example of corrective feedback is "You tried really hard but you need to bend your knees." Phrase corrective feedback positively and try to avoid the use of the word *no*.

JOHNNY completed a trial of throwing the ball overhand, but he did not step forward onto his opposite foot. Lin, the paraeducator, said, "Not quite right. Johnny, you have to step forward on this foot. Watch me," and then demonstrated. She asked Johnny, "Where is this foot?", and touched Johnny's opposite leg. Johnny indicated that the opposite foot should be ahead of the foot on his throwing side. Lin said, "That's right, your opposite foot is on this side" (in front of the foot on the throwing side). Then she touched his opposite leg again.

Johnny's story illustrates several important points. First, the paraeducator used corrective feedback in a positive manner. Second, several

▶ By encouraging students to clap for themselves and others, para-educators help learners engage in positive reinforcement.

types of prompts (cues) are used. The paraeducator used a direct verbal prompt and modeled the skill for Johnny. Physical prompting was also used; in this case it was partial physical prompting. Refer to table 5.4 to help you further understand which types of prompts were used.

Fading refers to gradually eliminating prompts and reinforcers (Dunn et al., 1986). Ideally, the learner will learn to respond to natural cues in the environment, although for some learners, that will be impossible. Also, cues are necessary for classroom management. The paraeducator in the opening story, Mrs. Anderson, was able to discontinue use of physical guidance with Lars in delivering the bowling ball and reminded him to watch his peers perform the skills (modeling). In a real-life situation, fading would have occurred

over a longer period of time than this story indicated. Fading also refers to gradually decreasing use of reinforcers until the natural consequence is the reinforcer. Again, in a real-life setting, fading would take place over time; decreasing reinforcers too rapidly may undo what the students have learned to do. Reinforcement moves from being continual to intermittent (e.g., reinforcing every second time, then every third time). Care must be taken to move from continual reinforcement to intermittent.

Several different teaching styles are available to teachers and paraeducators. Muska Mosston (1966) identified a spectrum of teaching styles. Although Mosston's first book was written more than 35 years ago, his continuum of teaching styles is still found in his later publications and in today's physical education methods and adapted physical education textbooks. Mosston's teaching styles are command, task, reciprocal, small group, individual program, guided discovery, and problem solving. These teaching styles are arranged from the most amount of teacher control to the least, and each is appropriate under different circumstances. Physical education teachers should be able to incorporate these styles in their repertoire of teaching skills. The appropriateness of the style is related to content of the lesson. In addition, teachers have some leeway in using their personal preferences while using a variety of styles. Although the teaching styles are not arranged in a spectrum, Adapted Physical Education National Standards (APENS) (National Consortium for Physical Education and Recreation for Individuals with Disabilities [NCPERID], 1995) expect adapted physical education teachers to demonstrate competencies in each style. Paraeducators' roles are those of assisting and providing support. Styles are presented from most to least amount of teacher control in table 5.5.

Peer Tutoring

Another successful instructional strategy that teachers can incorporate in a physical education class is the use of peer tutors. Peer tutors are a select group of students who have expressed an interest in working with learners with disabilities. Peer tutoring is a program designed to benefit both

▶ TABLE 5.5	Mosston's Spectrum of Teaching Styles in Physical Education
Learning style	Description
Command	All aspects of lesson (e.g., objectives, order of activities, activities themselves, organizational patterns, and quality of performance—what the textbooks say) are predetermined by teacher ahead of time. Teacher explains and demonstrates skill, all learners try performing skill at same time, and teacher offers general feedback to whole class. This style has been used and overused in physical education classes and is good in situations when absolute safety is required and the teacher needs to control when learners perform (e.g., using a parachute, swimming [within ability groups], golf, and archery). Paraeducator provides support for learner in a class-within-a-class setting.
Task	Teacher plans all elements in command style except allows for individual differences in performance. Task cards are often used and feedback is specific to learners. This style works well with stations. Paraeducator assists learners in reading task cards, traveling from one station to another, and offering encouragement, support, and feedback.
Reciprocal	Uses partners who do not need to be of same ability levels. A goal of this style is that learner pairs have equal-status relationships. Paraeducator pairs up learners with and without disabilities. If there are an odd number of students, such as three rather than two, paraeducator puts these three students in their own group. Social interaction and feedback are more than in command and task styles. This style works well in crowded settings since one peer is performing while the other is watching.
Small group; individualized	Extension of reciprocal style; each member has a specific task (e.g., doer, observer, recorder) with roles rotating within small group. Learners should develop a sense of responsibility—it takes the onus off teacher and paraeducator and puts it on the group of learners. APENS (NCPERID, 1995) calls this style *individualized*. This style is based on learners' specific needs, lessons should be structured for success, stations are often used, and feedback is given to the learner. The major difference between small group and individualized is that individual recording methods are used for each learner with the individualized style to meet IEP requirements. Paraeducator works with learners at a station or moves with them from station to station.
Guided discovery	Teacher does not tell the answer. This style might be used when trying to emphasize getting height in a basic vertical jump or being able to dribble with either foot in a soccer unit. Paraeducator's role is to keep learners on task.
Problem solving	Often termed *movement approach* or *movement exploration,* emphasis is on process rather than end product. Teacher presents movement challenges to learners and any reasonable movement is a correct answer. Learners increase their movement vocabularies by moving to the challenges. Paraeducator assists learners in interpreting challenges and encouraging learners.

Note: Guided discovery and problem-solving styles are used with preschool through lower-elementary learners.

the student with a disability and the peer. Peer tutors provide extra attention, encouragement, and feedback that help students with disabilities to be successful. The peer tutor develops an understanding of various instructional strategies (e.g., verbal prompting, modeling, and feedback) and gains a greater appreciation and understanding of one or more disabilities.

Peer tutoring has developed from a national model program in physical education, Project PEOPEL (Physical Education Opportunity Program for Exceptional Learners) (Long, Irmer, Burkett, Glasenapp, & Odenkirk, 1980). Project PEOPEL was developed to assist high school learners with disabilities to have successful experiences in adapted physical education by training peer tutors to assist with instruction. Although Project PEOPEL is no longer receiving federal funding, many peer tutoring programs have evolved from Project PEOPEL and are being used in schools today. Lieberman and Houston-Wilson (2002) justify using a peer tutoring program.

▶ Peer tutoring is a special way of helping students with disabilities to be successful since peer tutors provide extra attention, encouragement, and feedback that help achieve goals.

However, we cannot forget the role of the paraeducator and the meaningful contributions that you make. Your interactions with peer tutors, learners with disabilities, and physical education teachers are invaluable.

Physical education teachers often rely on you, the paraeducator, to help collaborate with peer tutors and other students when working with learners with disabilities. As a paraeducator, you are a positive role model for all students. Through your leadership and personal qualities, all learners, especially those with disabilities, can continue to experience success.

Types of Peer Tutors

A peer tutoring program can consist of class-wide peer tutors (CWPTs) and cross-aged peer tutors (CAPTs). Using CWPTs is one way for all learners in a class to engage in one-on-one instruction, thereby increasing the amount of time for practicing skills and learning. According to Houston-Wilson, Lieberman, Horton, and Kasser (1997), this form of reciprocal teaching using role reversal, in which learners take turns being students and teachers, allows for greater cohesiveness among all learners. In addition, the CWPT model provides for

The benefits of a peer tutoring program for students with disabilities include increased frequency of instruction and learning of subject matter, as well as increased social skills and social interaction. Benefits to peer tutors are positive cooperative learning experiences, positive social interactions, and better understanding of both the learner and the learner's disability and ability levels. Peer tutors can also become strong advocates for learners with disabilities and might possibly seek a career in education. Gaustad (1993) noted that the benefits to the peer tutors are increased self-esteem and the knowledge that they are making a meaningful contribution to students with a disability.

Facts About Peer Tutoring

- Learners with disabilities need a smaller ratio of teacher to learner than do learners without disabilities.
- One-on-one instruction increases academic learning time (DePaepe, 1985; Webster, 1987).
- Tutors learn skills better than if they had not had the opportunity to teach them (Briggs, 1975).
- Peer tutoring increases leadership experience among tutors (Rink, 1998).
- Peer tutoring stimulates socialization among peers.
- Cooperative learning experiences promote more interpersonal attention between learners with and without disabilities, higher self-esteem, and greater empathy on the part of all children (Johnson & Johnson, 1983).
- Participation together as partners and equals encourages positive relationships (Sinibaldi, 2001).

greater social interaction, enhanced communication skills, and greater appreciation of peers with and without disabilities. Reddy et al. (1999) have pointed out that there is a growing trend toward the implementation of CWPTs because teachers have an increased awareness of all learners' abilities and the positive effect they can have on each other.

Paraeducators can play an important role in the monitoring and assisting of CWPTs. While the peer tutors are interacting with learners with disabilities, the paraeducator can assist with instruction, record data, and maintain a positive learning environment while helping all students stay engaged in class activities, as in the following example.

MRS. Conner, a paraeducator, was monitoring a group of students as they practiced the serve in volleyball. Mary, a student with cerebral palsy who used a wheelchair, was excited about participating with her friends in volleyball. However, Mary was having difficulty striking the ball correctly in order to get it over the net. Mrs. Conner intervened and had two CWPTs take turns helping Mary strike the ball. In addition, Mary moved closer to the net so that she could serve the ball over the net.

In the previous example, with assistance from the paraeducator, all learners were engaged in helping Mary to become more successful when participating in volleyball. This collaborative effort by the paraeducator and CWPTs demonstrates how a successful learning experience can be achieved.

With CAPTs, tutors are older than learners with disabilities. This form of peer tutoring has strong implications for younger students. According to Sherrill (1993), CAPTs play an important role when providing instruction for elementary schools as physical education teacher assistants. One advantage of CAPTs is that the tutor is more advanced in the subject matter than the learner with disabilities. According to Block (1995), the best peer tutors tend to be older students who are mature and responsible and have expressed an interest in working with learners with disabilities. CAPTs can play an important role to students with disabilities while improving their own teaching skills. Winnick (2005) has pointed out that CAPTs increase their learning experiences along with being positive role

models for younger children. Paraeducators who have an opportunity to monitor CAPTs can ensure that they don't communicate false information or errors. A paraeducator can often provide valuable information to a CAPT regarding a learner with disabilities, as in the following example.

CHRISTINA, a high school CAPT, was assigned to help Tonya, a child with autism at an elementary school. Christina was excited about working with Tonya on one of her IEP objectives, catching a softball. However, Christina was having difficulty with Tonya staying on task and finishing the skill. Mrs. Roberts, a paraeducator, had worked with Tonya for the past 3 years and thus had a good understanding

▶ By working with CAPTs, paraeducators are helping the CAPTs gain valuable teaching abilities and are helping to offer the students an opportunity to work with tutors with advanced knowledge of the subject matter.

of instructional strategies that were effective in helping Tonya stay focused during class activities. Mrs. Roberts intervened and provided specific instructional strategies that directly related to Tonya. This allowed Christina to redirect Tonya's behavior and complete the assignment.

As in the story about Christina and Tonya, paraeducators who have instructional strategies specific to a learner with disabilities can be instrumental to the teacher and peer tutor when working with the learner.

Peer tutors can be recruited from a variety of sources, ranging from higher grade levels, other same-age classes, or from the teacher's own class. Houston-Wilson et al. (1997) have suggested that any child who expresses an interest to serve as a peer tutor would be preferred. Lieberman, Newcomer, McCubbin, and Dalrymple (1997) have suggested that peer tutors are an inexpensive way to help learners with disabilities experience success in general physical education. Block, Oberweiser, and Bain (1995) recommend that peer tutors be mature individuals who are capable of handling the responsibilities outlined in the peer tutoring program and are willing to work with students with a disability.

Paraeducators can assist in the process of selecting qualified learners to become peer tutors. As a paraeducator, you are exposed to a variety of students throughout the day. You have the ability to identify candidates for the peer tutoring program who are

- mature individuals capable of handling the responsibilities of working one on one with students different from themselves,
- able to communicate with verbal and non-verbal skills,
- able to participate in classes designed for learners with disabilities,
- able to follow the teacher's directions well,
- flexible with their schedule without being distracted from other school objectives, and
- able to attend school on a regular basis.

MRS. Barnes, a paraeducator, had been assigned to assist Tim, a learner with disabilities, in making sure he was able to maneu-

ver his wheelchair through the lunch line to pay for his lunch. As the week progressed and Tim waited in line, Mrs. Barnes noticed that Travis and Jacob had become friendly with Tim and helped him with his lunch selection. Mrs. Barnes invited both Travis and Jacob to join them at their table. Throughout the next few weeks, Travis and Jacob made a point of helping Tim and sitting with him during their lunch period. Mrs. Barnes enjoyed watching the friendship grow between Tim, Travis, and Jacob as the weeks passed. Travis and Jacob had good social and communication skills and would be excellent candidates for the peer tutoring program. Mrs. Barnes talked to Travis and Jacob about the peer tutoring program that assisted learners with disabilities in physical education. Both Travis and Jacob were eager to sign up for the program and went to a workshop on peer tutoring that was offered after school.

As a paraeducator, you have many opportunities throughout the day to gather valuable information on interested learners who want to become peer tutors. Miller and Cordova (2002) noted that when learners become engaged in a peer tutor program and make direct social contact with learners with disabilities, they develop positive attitudes toward learners with disabilities. Your contribution to the development of a peer tutoring program is instrumental in providing experiences of success for learners with disabilities.

Training Peer Tutors

One important factor in the training process of a peer tutor is the ability of the teacher to find an adequate amount of time throughout the day to incorporate training. Gartner and Riessman (1993) have suggested taking careful consideration during the preparation to train peer tutors and the ongoing reflection on the tutoring process. Lieberman and Houston-Wilson (2002, p. 80) stated that "peer tutoring training can take up to an hour or more, depending on the age of the tutor, the child's disability and the unit of instruction." Paraeducators with past experience in assisting teacher and peer tutors can take part in the training process of peer tutors. Oftentimes, a paraeducator has developed specific instructional strategies relating to learners with disabilities. These instructional strategies generally coincide with instructional strategies that are taught to peer tutors. You can take advantage of their experiences and assist in instruction of prospective peer tutors, ultimately benefiting the student with disabilities. Often there is marked improvement in the following areas:

- Disability awareness
- Communication techniques
- Teaching strategies
- Skill analysis
- Reinforcement techniques

Once established, the benefits of a peer tutoring program will be recognized when all learners demonstrate increased social skills, increased time on task, and improved communication skills and work habits.

Administered correctly, peer tutoring can be a valuable instructional strategy that helps teachers and paraeducators when assisting learners with disabilities in general physical education. Peer tutors allow for greater flexibility over the traditional teacher-centered model. However, recruiting, training, and overseeing peer tutors require a great deal of time and attention in order for peer tutoring to be successful. Physical education teachers and paraeducators can share in the responsibility of training peer tutors. Once established, the gains derived from a quality peer tutoring program will have a significant impact on the assistance provided to all learners in general physical education.

Summary

The purpose of this chapter was to present instructional strategies for paraeducators to use with their students in physical education settings. Paraeducators are valuable members of their learners' education teams and play an important role in the education of learners with disabilities. Having an understanding of instructional strategies should assist you in working with your students in physical education and in teaming with adapted physical education teachers, general physical education teachers, and special education teachers. You have been exposed to levels of support, adaptations and modifications, teaching techniques, and working with peer tutors. A collaborative effort using the strategies discussed here will result in a positive learning environment for everyone.

CHAPTER 6

Assessment

Lauren Lieberman and Carin Mulawka

Guiding Questions

▶ Name and describe three areas of assessment.

▶ Name and describe two types of tests.

▶ Name three purposes of assessment.

▶ What is the paraeducator's role in the assessment process?

▶ Describe five of the seven steps in collecting data.

ETHAN was an enthusiastic 2nd grader who had Fragile X Syndrome. He had a paraeducator, Ms. Sereno, who had been with him since kindergarten. Ethan typically went to physical education by himself because he was very active, and Ms. Sereno felt he did not need any support in this area. The truth was that Ethan was active, but he rarely performed the skills that the teacher asked the students to do. For example, when she asked them to skip, Ethan would run; when she asked them to hop, Ethan would jump. It was not because he had a behavior problem; rather, he did not always know exactly how to do the activity or that the skill he was performing was wrong.

The physical education teacher, Mrs. Fittipauldi, was in her second year of teaching and enjoyed the school, the support staff, and the administration. Mrs. Fittipauldi wanted to be sure she was teaching to the needs of the students, so she planned on assessing all the students using the Test of Gross Motor Development II (TGMD II) at the beginning of the school year. Mrs. Fittipauldi discovered early on that she was having a hard time obtaining all the information she needed from her class by herself. She also realized that in Ethan's case, he was capable of performing the skills, but he did not have enough instruction and feedback to do them correctly. Mrs. Fittipauldi approached Ms. Sereno to ask her if she could come to physical education and assist with administration of the TGMD II. Ms. Sereno was more than willing to help.

During two short 20-minute sessions after school, Mrs. Fittipauldi taught Ms. Sereno what to look for in several of the object-control skills. Because of the extra help, Mrs. Fittipauldi was able to assess most of the class on object-control skills the next time they had class. Ms. Sereno was also able to know that Ethan understood each skill that was assessed, ensuring that she was getting accurate information on his assessment. The next class Ms. Sereno recorded locomotor skill scores and again ensured that Ethan was performing to the best of his ability. Ms. Sereno realized how helpful she had been in physical education and that she was truly needed in the physical education setting. When Mrs. Fittipauldi asked her to continue coming to physical education, she was enthusiastic. Ms. Sereno helped determine percentile scores from the raw scores for the TGMD II, and she helped with rubric assessments during units on gymnastics, dance, and obstacle courses and during fitness testing at the end of the year. Ms. Sereno realized that in order to make sure that Ethan was tested on his best ability and to assist Mrs. Fittipauldi, she needed to be an active member of the physical education program. This was truly a win–win situation.

Introduction

As can be seen in the opening scenario, conducting assessments takes a lot of time, energy, and personnel. It is important to conduct well-planned and methodical assessments in order to make sure you get the most reliable information from the students, and this is a very difficult task. In order to obtain the most productive assessment of all students, the paraeducator must be involved. This chapter will discuss types of assessments, paraeducators' roles in assessment, and a variety of strategies for collecting data.

Areas to Assess

Assessment is extremely important in all areas of education, especially physical education. Assessment should be a major part of the curriculum in order for educators to be accountable for student learning. Students can be assessed in many areas within physical education. In physical education, the goal is to teach the whole student. There are three domains of behavior that can be assessed: the psychomotor domain, the cognitive domain, and the affective domain (see table 6.1 on page 63). In the opening scenario, Mrs. Fittipauldi was testing Ethan on the psychomotor domain.

The psychomotor domain can be defined as a student's set of motor skills. Within the psychomotor domain, students' fitness can be assessed, which includes flexibility, cardiovascular endurance, body mass index (if they are too fat or too thin), muscular strength, and muscular endurance. Another area of psychomotor assessment is locomotor skills, such as hopping, skipping, jumping, or galloping. Students can also be assessed on object-

▶ Sport skills are an area of the psychomotor domain that can easily be assessed by paraeducators.

specific activities, strategies for a certain game, rules for different sports, history of a specific activity or sport, or dimensions of a court or field. The paraeducator may be asked to read the test to the student, assist in recording the student's answers, or help the student understand certain questions on the test.

Last, students may be assessed on the affective domain. Affective behaviors are attributes such as teamwork, cooperation, enjoyment, appreciation, and commitment. Although these traits or behaviors may be more abstract or subjective, they are often part of a holistic approach to assessment. In this case, the paraeducator may be asked to rate a student's cooperation, assist in determining a teamwork score on a Likert scale (e.g., 1-5), or help students focus during a unit in order to ensure appreciation.

Although there are three domains of behavior, most teachers assess only one domain at a time per unit. Some teachers may only use the psychomotor domain in physical education. In any case, it is extremely important for the paraeducator to assist the teacher in any way necessary. Without assessment information, there is no accountability for student learning. Following are more purposes of assessment in physical education.

control skills, such as batting, kicking, throwing, catching, or rolling, and they may be assessed on sport skills, such as basketball offense and defense, volleyball, tennis, aquatics, or golf.

Students may also be assessed on their cognitive skills. These tests assess the students' knowledge in certain areas such as types of muscles used in

Purposes of Assessment

Purposes of assessment are vast and far reaching. As mentioned earlier, a major reason to assess is to hold the teacher, student, and paraeducator accountable for learning. Just as it is imperative to show improvement in other academic areas, it

▶ **TABLE 6.1   Domains of Assessment**

Areas to be assessed	What it assesses	Examples
Psychomotor test	Motor ability	Running, hopping, jumping, throwing, catching, rolling, fitness activities
Cognitive tests	Knowledge	Specific activities, types of muscles used, strategies, rules, history
Affective tests	Behaviors or attitudes	Teamwork, cooperation, enjoyment, appreciation, commitment

is also imperative to document improvement in physical education.

Another major purpose of assessment is to determine if the student with a disability is eligible for adapted physical education. Adapted physical education is physical education modified to meet the unique needs of the student. A thorough assessment will give enough information to determine if students need their physical education modified to meet their needs. Adapted physical education is the service to the student, not the placement. In other words, adapted physical education can be delivered in inclusive or separate settings. Assessment will also help determine if the student should be taught in the general physical education class with certain supports, a separate class, or a combination of both. This is called the *placement* of the student with the disability.

Assessing the students gives the teacher a starting block for program development. The strengths and weaknesses determined by assessment help the instructor create the program and make sure that the students are not too challenged or bored by the curriculum. In the opening scenario, Ethan and his class were being assessed on the TGMD II, which assesses gross motor skills. Mrs. Fittipauldi took the scores of the students and determined areas of weakness to target in her curriculum for the year. Without assessment, appropriate program development may not be possible.

Assessment conducted throughout the year provides instructors with information on where the students have been, where they are currently, and where they are going. This information gives instructors criteria to determine if they have improved during each unit and if they have met their objectives and goals. If they have not met their goals, assessment helps determine how far they are from reaching each goal. This critical part of assessment is the basis for the IEP development and implementation discussed in chapter 7.

When students are involved in physical education without assessment, they are much less motivated than when they experience physical education while being assessed. For this reason, motivation is a major reason why students are assessed. For example, Sarah was a student in Ethan's class. She was involved in her gymnastics unit and was going through the motions of tumbling and the balance beam. Once the teacher started assessing using the rubrics, Sarah pushed herself and set goals for the next class. This enthusiasm and goal setting only occurred after she knew her performance counted and was being recorded.

Purposes of Assessment

- Accountability
- Eligibility for services
- Placement
- Program development
- Objectives and goals
- Motivation

Types of Assessment

Standardized tests or traditional assessments are tests that analyze the performance of students in controlled environments (Short, 2005). The testing environment for standardized tests is very structured and rigid (Kasser & Lytle, 2005). The results of these tests are most often compared to the norm of the population and a percentage is then assigned to the score. An example of a traditional assessment would be a tennis test where the learner hit forehands crosscourt from a feeder 10 times in a row and the correct strokes are counted. The results of standardized tests most often are used to determine eligibility for services, placement decisions (e.g., separate physical education, inclusive physical education), and often programming decisions. The TGMD II discussed in the opening scenario can be used for placement. If students like Ethan score below a certain percentile or a specific standard, they may be eligible for separate physical education classes.

Standardized tests are most often used in contrived environments such as the corner of a gymnasium and not in a real game situation. For example, when assessing volleyball using a standard assessment, the ball may be served or fed to the students and they execute a skill they use in a game. On the other hand, authentic assessments are used in a natural class setting, such as recording the performance of students during a game or activity situation. This approach closely links assessment to instruction because it gives the teacher information on the student's strengths and weaknesses in the current activity (Lieberman & Houston-Wilson, 2002; Short, 2005). An example of an authentic assessment is an assessment of volleyball skills where students are evaluated on the number of times they execute a skill appropriately in a game situation. The recording sheet for this assessment may look like table 6.2.

TABLE 6.2 Authentic Assessment for Volleyball Skills

Skill	Correct form	Incorrect form
Bump	11111	11
Set	11	1111
Spike	111	1

Using a checklist such as the one in table 6.2 may be difficult for a teacher without the help of the paraeducator or peer tutors. In the case of an 11th-grade student with cerebral palsy named Jacinta, the paraeducator conducted most of her assessments during her physical education class. Jacinta also had a trained peer tutor who knew her strengths and abilities. The paraeducator taught Jacinta's peer tutor how to use the rubric and recording sheet for each unit, and the paraeducator and the peer tutor took turns assessing Jacinta with the class recording sheet.

Another type of assessment is a rubric, or a multilevel assessment system that matches performance to specific criteria that are associated with a number or level of skill. See table 6.3 for a sample rubric.

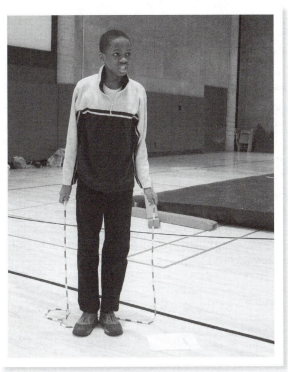

▶ With instruction from paraeducators, students can use rubrics, such as the jump rope rubric, to help assess themselves.

TABLE 6.3 Sample Jump Rope Rubric

Rubric level and color	Rubric descriptors
1—red	Student will crawl, roll, walk, and jump over a rope placed up to 1 foot (30 centimeters) off the ground.
2—orange	Student will step or jump forward over a rope placed 1 foot (30 centimeters) off the ground, either stationary or swinging.
3—yellow	Student will bring rope over head with arms and step or roll over rope once.
4—green	Student will bring rope over head with arms and step or roll over rope 2-20 times.
5—blue	Student will jump rope, swinging rope over head backward, 1-20 times.
6—indigo	Student will jump rope to music forward, backward, crisscross, for 1-5 minutes.
7—violet	Student will jump rope to music, either alone or with a partner, for 6-20 minutes.
Specific adaptations	

Adapted, by permission, from L. Lieberman and C. Houston-Wilson, 2002, *Strategies for inclusion: A handbook for physical educators* (Champaign, IL: Human Kinetics), 112.

Another assessment tool similar to a rubric is a task analysis. Task analysis is the process of taking a skill and breaking it down into smaller steps. This information can be made into a checklist to determine what parts of a skill are mastered and what parts are not. See table 6.4 for a sample task analysis.

In table 6.4, the task analysis is set up in a way that gives the teacher information about the level of support a student may need during a skill. It asks if the student can complete the skill independently with just verbal assistance or with partial physical assistance, or if the student needs total assistance to complete the task. It is assumed that the instructor will use instruction, demonstration, and modeling during instruction. Some task analyses are more complex, and some are even simpler, asking only if a skill component is present or not.

The TGMD II, used by Ms. Sereno with Ethan at the beginning of this chapter, is a task analysis. In the case of this test, a point was given each time a student mastered a skill component.

Another assessment strategy is the use of portfolios. A portfolio is documentation of student work through work samples such as rubrics, assessments, documented routines, test results, videotapes, teacher observations, peer ratings, checklists, journals, and logs (Short, 2005). Some schools store these materials in individual student boxes, some use folders, and some use electronic methods. One of the most difficult tasks when using portfolios is collection and distribution of materials. This is a task that the paraeducator can assist with, truly supporting the physical educator. The following is a list of sample portfolio items:

Rubrics	Test results
Assessments	Teacher observations
Documented routines	Peer ratings
Videotapes	Checklists
Journals	Logs

▶ **TABLE 6.4 Sample Badminton Task Analysis**

Skill	Independently	Partial physical assistance	Total physical assistance
Shoulder to the net			
Hold birdie with nondominant hand in front of same-side foot			
Step with nondominant foot			
Backswing with racket in dominant hand			
Contact birdie in front of front foot with racket			
Follow through with racket			

It would be safe to say that physical educators perform assessments in most of the areas depicted within the definition of physical education given in the IDEA law (i.e., physical and motor fitness; fundamental motor skills; and skills for individual sports, group games, aquatics, and rhythms). In order to conduct these assessments, physical educators must consider several variables that influence the implementation of a particular test. Variables to consider during testing administration might be location, amount of equipment needed, number of students to be tested during a particular session, cues or prompts needed to convey instructions for the test, and the amount of time needed to conduct the test.

All of these considerations are compounded when attempting to test students with and without disabilities in the same setting. For example, in the opening scenario Mrs. Fittipauldi was setting up the environment for the TGMD II. For object control she needed batting, throwing, rolling, catching, and kicking stations. Ms. Sereno was very helpful in setting up and taking down the equipment. With the help of Ms. Sereno and one other paraeducator, it only took a few minutes to set up the equipment.

Now that the purpose of assessment and some popular assessments used are understood, we will discuss the role of the paraeducator in the assessment process.

Paraeducators' Role in Assessment

As stated earlier, assessment is vital in physical education; however, it is difficult for the physical education teacher to assess the entire class without assistance. The paraeducator plays a critical role in obtaining input, data, and information on student performance. It is not always easy to analyze skills, but teachers will explain clearly what they are looking for in a given assessment. There are several steps in collecting data for assessment in physical education. Table 6.5 offers some suggestions of how paraeducators can assist with the assessment process for fitness.

The many steps of data collection include the following:

Step 1: Learn the purpose of the assessment. For example, if you understand what the assessment is measuring, it will be easier to collect correct information.

▶ **TABLE 6.5 Role of Paraeducators During Assessment**

Assessment area	Component	Paraeducator's role in assessment
Physical fitness	Cardiovascular endurance	Record number of laps completed on a timed distance run. Help student add or remove heart rate monitors if used. Assume various positions on the track to serve as a motivator or shout encouragement during test.
Physical fitness	Muscular endurance, strength (upper body)	Secure feet of student during curl-up or sit-up testing. Take position next to student for pull-up or suspended arm hang to help with safety.
Fundamental motor skills	Throw, catch, run, jump, kick	If distances need to be modified for throwing, catching, or kicking tests, stand in position to enforce the location of the modified distance. If distances for running need to be modified, stand in position to mark the beginning or end of the run. Assist in getting the student into the correct position for the task.
Dance	Dance steps and sequence	Prompt the students with different cues to get the steps or sequence. Perform the assessment off to the side to reduce extraneous stimuli.
Cognitive knowledge	Written tests	Read test questions to the student. Write down the student's responses to the questions.

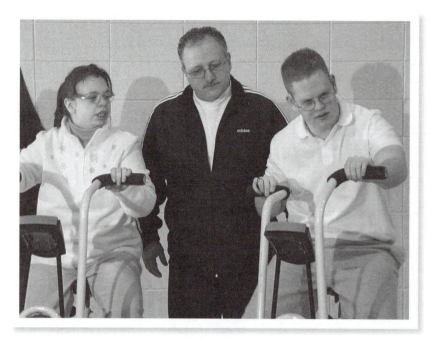

▶ Paraeducators can assess students one on one during station work or with peers.

in an environment where the devices should be removed, such as a pool.)

Step 4: Learn the appropriate terminology to use with the test that the students will understand (Seaman, Depauw, Morton, & Omoto, 2003). For example, the TGMD II used with Ethan's class called for the nonsupported leg to be bent to 90° during a run. If you do not understand what this means, ask the teacher to show you an example so you are accurately recording the data.

Step 5: Assist the teacher with setting up the testing environment. Equipment should be arranged near the testing station but should not distract the student (Auxter, Pyfer, & Huettig, 2005). Many times an abundance of equipment is needed for assessment (e.g., tennis rackets, mats, balls), and your assistance will increase the amount of time spent in testing.

Step 2: Communicate with teachers about your role regarding assessment. Make sure you have time to practice and that you know what you are looking for in skill and performance related to scoring.

Step 3: Discuss with the teacher what modifications, if any, must be made for your student (Sherrill, 2004). Often the paraeducator knows the student with a disability better than the teacher does. Your input will ensure that the student is being fairly assessed. (Note: If students use braces, orthotics, or a wheelchair for functional use, they should be assessed while using these devices, unless, of course, they are

Step 6: Collect data in physical education for students with and without disabilities. Table 6.6 will allow you to understand the various ways you can assist in collecting data.

Step 7: Interpreting the data is an important step in assessment. This step must be completed shortly after collecting the data so that it is easier to remember student performance (Auxter et al., 2005). You may be asked to assist with data analysis in several ways. See table 6.7 for data analysis strategies and examples of each.

▶ TABLE 6.6 Methods to Collect Data for Assessment	
1:1	The student with the disability can be assessed by the instructor or the paraeducator on a one-to-one basis.
Small group	The paraeducator can be responsible for collecting the data for a small group of students in the class. The students may have disabilities, but they do not have to have a disability in order for the paraeducator to assess them; it is just easier to work with a group of students with similar abilities (e.g., pull-ups).
Entire class	The physical educator may expect the paraeducator to assist with collecting data for the entire class. For example, if the class has a timed swim, you may be asked to record the number of laps that each student swims.

Stations	The entire assessment may be spread out throughout the gymnasium or outdoor area with each test item being a different station. You may be asked to record data at one or two specific stations.
Peer to peer	The students may be asked to assess each other. Your job would be to monitor the data collecting of the peers, answer questions, and ensure they are collecting data correctly.
Combination of the previous strategies	In some cases a combination of two or more collection strategies may be used. For example, the test may be divided into stations, and the students assess each other while you either monitor everyone or record data at one station.
Collecting and distributing portfolios	If the class uses portfolio assessments, you may be asked to distribute and collect portfolios. You may also be asked to assist your students with their data recording for their portfolio.
Recording data	Many schools record their assessment data on a personal digital assistant (PDA) for ease of interpretation. If your school uses a PDA, your teacher will instruct you on how to record the information. If you do not use a PDA, you may use a recording sheet with a pencil. The data may be transferred later to computer software.
Videotape	In some cases you may be asked to videotape the class and record the performance of the student with the disability or a group of students.
Checklist	The instructor may give you a checklist and explain the performance criteria to look for under each category. You will then check the appropriate boxes.
Rating scale	The instructor may give you a rating scale and explain the performance criteria to look for under each level of achievement. You will then check the appropriate level.
Rubric	You may be given a rubric to follow and observe each level that is accomplished and record performance.
Description	In some cases students may not be able to be assessed using the previous strategies. They may have a severe behavior disability, physical disability, or both. In such cases it may be easier to describe performance in a narrative of what they can do relating to the area of assessment the teacher is focusing on.

▶ **TABLE 6.7 Strategies for Data Analysis**

Data analysis strategies	Examples
Rerecording data from class	Copying data from your recording sheet onto a master document
Transferring data to a computer	Typing student scores from your recording sheet onto a spreadsheet or file on the computer
Creating a poster or a bulletin board of assessment results	Using the assessment results as motivation for students by creating a colorful bulletin board or poster of their results
Taking the data and assisting in writing the present level of performance for the IEP	Working with the teacher to describe the student's performance for use in the IEP
Assisting with creating goals and objectives for the student with the disability	Using the assessment results, you and the teacher determine strengths and weaknesses of the student to create the student's goals and objectives for class
Assisting with the program development for the student with the disability	Using the assessment results, you and the teacher develop a program for your student

Summary

Assessment in physical education is necessary in order to be accountable for student learning. Without assessment, teachers would not know what to teach or if what they taught was learned. Conducting assessments is a tedious and often time-consuming task. With the assistance of the paraeducator in each phase of the assessment process, testing can be thorough, accurate, easy to understand, and even fun.

CHAPTER 7

Individual Education Programs

Ellen Kowalski

Guiding Questions

▶ What is an individual education program (IEP)?

▶ What are the components of the IEP?

▶ How can the paraeducator assist in the development of the IEP?

▶ What is the role of the paraeducator in the implementation of the IEP?

▶ How can paraeducators assist with improving social behaviors?

▶ How can paraeducators help implement transition programs into the community for high school students and help educate parents?

JAVIER was in the 3rd grade and had Down syndrome. He was very social and enjoyed interaction with his peers, and he had a para-educator named Maria who was well meaning and followed him around all the time. His IEP goals were socialization, fundamental motor skills, and eye–hand coordination (object-control skills). His special education teacher, Ms. Ellis, did not believe he could accomplish these goals and wanted him placed in the segregated setting with students with severe disabilities. Ms. Mahoney, the elementary physical educator, knew that Javier did not belong in the segregated class but was having difficulty meeting his goals and objectives for physical education because the class was quite large. With the help of Maria and some creativity, Ms. Mahoney worked hard to ensure that Javier's goals and objectives would be met within his general physical education class. The IEP was a critical component and excellent guide for the whole team to ensure Javier's specific needs were met.

Introduction

The individual education program, commonly known as the IEP, is critical because it serves as the centerpiece of the education of students with disabilities. As seen in the above scenario, even in a complicated situation, the IEP guided the teachers and paraeducator to meet the student's specific needs. The paraeducator also plays a key role in the development of the IEP and its implementation into the physical education curriculum. This chapter will cover all aspects of your involvement in the IEP process and program development in physical education.

Getting Started With the Individual Education Program

According to IDEA, all students with disabilities from ages 3 to 21 must have an IEP (Federal Register, 1999). The IEP is a written document that is developed to make sure that each child with a disability receives quality educational programming (Lieberman & Houston-Wilson, 2002). It is essentially a blueprint or action plan for the student's education for the year and also serves as a guide

and an accountability tool for teachers, specialists, school administrators, and parents (Seaman, DePauw, Morton, & Omoto, 2003).

There are different types of IEPs. The one mainly discussed in this chapter is the general IEP, developed for school-aged children from 3 to 21 years old. When students with disabilities enter high school, the IEP changes slightly so that the goals and objectives focus on the students' transition into the community after graduation from high school (Seaman et al., 2003). This type of IEP, for students aged 14 and older, is called an *individual transition plan* (ITP). An IEP for infants and toddlers (birth to age 3) receiving early intervention services is called an *individual family service plan* (IFSP), where the focus is on the family and home as the educational setting.

The IEP Process

The development of an IEP involves several people to make sure that it is tailored to the needs of the individual student. IDEA requires a minimum number of people on a multidisciplinary IEP team: the student, student's parents, teachers, administrators, and specialists. An IEP is not something that is fixed or set in stone, but a living, breathing document that is continually changing and being updated based on changing circumstances (Auxter, Pyfer, & Heuttig, 2005; Seaman et al., 2003). Although some procedures vary from state to state, the steps involved in developing an IEP are essentially the same. Within this process there are several steps that involve the paraeducator, and the paraeducator plays a critical role in assisting the physical and adapted physical education teachers in the IEP process, from referral to program implementation. To understand your role in the development and implementation of the IEP, you must first understand the components of the IEP and the steps in the IEP process.

Steps in the IEP Process

1. Referral
2. Assessment
3. Present level of performance (PLP)
4. Annual goals
5. Short-term instructional objectives

6. Program implementation

7. Review and update

Referral

If a student does not already have an IEP, referral is the first step in the IEP process. Any professional staff member, including the paraeducator or a parent who suspects that a student might have a disability, may refer that student for an evaluation. Because you often have the most contact with students with disabilities, you can be instrumental in communicating your observations of children who may need the help of an IEP. Once it is determined through assessment that a student is eligible for special services and parents give written consent, the IEP is developed.

Assessment

Assessment is a crucial step in the IEP process because it provides the starting point for developing the present level of performance (PLP) (see the following step). In order to develop a PLP that describes the unique needs of a student with a disability, the student must be assessed in as many content areas of physical education as possible (motor skills, fitness, aquatics, and so on). However, parents must first receive notification and give written consent for their child to be tested. As the paraeducator, you are instrumental in this step of the process because you can assist the physical or adapted physical education teacher in gathering assessment data (described in chapter 6) for the PLP, which is particularly difficult in large classes like the one described in this chapter's opening scenario.

Present Level of Performance

Based on information compiled from assessment data and observations by teachers and specialists, the IEP team then writes a PLP, which is a thorough description of a student's current motor abilities, including strengths and weaknesses. The description of the student's performance should be written in objective and observable terms so that it clearly and accurately reflects what the student is able to demonstrate and accomplish at the time. However, the PLP is more than simply listing assessment data; it involves qualitative information based on observation. Because you have direct contact with the student, your obser-

vations and feedback can add to assessment data in the PLP, thus giving a more complete picture of the student. The PLP is an important step because it helps the teachers to identify appropriate goals and objectives and it provides documentation justifying why certain goals for a student are selected. For example, Javier, the 3rd grader with Down syndrome described in the opening scenario, is able to demonstrate an overhand throwing pattern to a partner 5 feet (1.5 meters) away three out of five attempts.

Annual Goals

From the student's PLP, appropriate annual goals are selected. Annual goals are broad statements that target general areas of a student's PLP that need to be improved. Annual goals must clearly relate to information described in the student's present PLP and should be selected from the weaknesses, not the strengths. For example, if a student's PLP only addressed information on balance, eye–foot coordination, and eye–hand coordination, it would be unsuitable to write an annual goal for fitness. It would also be inappropriate to select the same annual goal if fitness was described as one of the student's strengths (Short, 2005).

Sometimes students with disabilities have multiple weaknesses, making it difficult to know what to focus on in the student's educational program. Identifying two or three goals instead of trying to work on everything helps the teacher prioritize the most important weaknesses that a student needs to improve. For example, because Javier's paraeducator works directly with Javier and helped collect assessment data for the PLP, she can assist the physical educator in selecting the most appropriate goals for Javier to work on. A sample annual goal could be Javier demonstrating a mature overhand throwing pattern for a distance of 15 feet (4.5 meters) in 8 out of 10 attempts by June. (Note that although this goal is specific and measurable, some districts elect to write annual goals that are broadly stated.)

Short-Term Instructional Objectives

Short-term instructional objectives are written for each annual goal identified on a student's IEP. Short-term objectives are small, intermediate steps designed to help the student work toward achieving each annual goal. These objectives are important because they provide a direct link between the PLP (where the student is) and the outcome stated in the annual goal (where the student wants to go). Short-term objectives should be challenging yet realistically achievable (Lieberman & Houston-Wilson, 2002). As the paraeducator, you can provide valuable input to the physical education teacher and assist in creating these challenging yet achievable objectives.

Short-term objectives are stated as observable, measurable behaviors. *Observable* means behaviors or actions that you can see such as kicking, balance, throwing, and running. Behaviors that are not observable are described by words such as *know, feel,* and *understand.* Each short-term objective has three parts. The first part identifies what performance or action (e.g., throw, catch, kick, balance) needs to be developed or changed. The second part consists of the conditions, which describe how the skill will be developed. The way the action is performed or the situation the action is performed in makes a big difference in changing the difficulty of the objective. This part includes information about the environment, type of equipment, distance, and so on. For example, the conditions would specify if the action performed is in the gymnasium or on the field. An object thrown might be a beanbag, tennis ball, playground ball, or beach ball, or a gallop may be on the floor, on a line on the floor, or on a balance beam. Other information might include distance, speed, amount of weight, and so on.

The third part of a short-term objective is the criterion. A criterion is a measure of success, or how well the action needs to be performed (Sherrill, 2004; Short, 2005), such as counting the number of times a skill is performed correctly, timing for speed, or measuring the distance jumped. There are two ways to measure success: quantitative measures and qualitative measures. Quantitative measures reflect a concrete number such as distance, time, or number of times an action is performed (such as 8 out of 10 times). Qualitative measures reflect which aspects of an action are performed correctly.

Examples of short-term objectives for Javier could include the following:

- using a tennis ball, Javier will be able to hit a 3- × 3-foot (1- × 1-meter) target from

6 feet (2 meters) away, demonstrating an overhand throw, in 8 out of 10 attempts by November;

- using a tennis ball, Javier will be able to hit a 3- × 3-foot (1- × 1-meter) target from 10 feet (3 meters) away, demonstrating an overhand throw while stepping with the opposite foot, in 8 out of 10 attempts by March; and

- using a tennis ball, Javier will be able to hit a 3- × 3-foot (1- × 1-meter) target from 15 feet (4.5 meters) away, demonstrating an overhand throw while stepping with the opposite foot, in 8 out of 10 attempts by June.

HOW SHORT-TERM OBJECTIVES HELP PHYSICAL EDUCATORS TEACH STUDENTS WITH DISABILITIES

1. Short-term objectives help teachers to be more aware of a student's strengths and weaknesses and develop a program based on the student's individual needs. Knowing the short-term objectives helps the teacher in selecting and designing creative activities that work on a student's targeted goals within the curriculum.
2. Short-term objectives help teachers modify their existing units, lesson plans, and activities in order to connect more directly with the student's short-term objectives.
3. Short-term objectives help teachers determine if a student is making progress toward a targeted goal area or if a goal or objective needs to be changed (Lieberman & Houston-Wilson, 2002).
4. Short-term objectives can motivate students. If a teacher or paraeducator shares the short-term objectives with students, the students can clearly see if they are making progress and may be motivated to work hard to meet the objectives.

Program Implementation

Using the student's individual short-term objectives as a guide, the physical educator creates an instructional program based on the student's individual needs. Teachers can incorporate a student's targeted goals and short-term objectives into their units, lesson plans, and activities in two ways: during activity selection (because one activity might challenge both the student's objective plus the general class objective) and by modifying existing activities or creating new activities. For example, let's say partners are bouncing and catching an 8-inch (20-centimeter) playground ball with increasing distance. The teacher can easily add an action (toss) and different types of balls. This modification helps all students work on ball-handling skills and includes one student's short-term instructional objective. As the paraeducator, you can be instrumental in coming up with ideas for modifying activities and incorporating your student's goals and objectives into a variety of games and activities.

Review and Update

Though a student's IEP may be reviewed at any time, it must be evaluated at least annually. This is when the IEP team is provided with information describing how much progress has been made toward the student's objectives and goals. One required component of the IEP is the procedures for evaluation and parental report. This means that every IEP must identify the specific assessment instruments that were used to develop the student's PLP. There must be a description of how the student's progress toward the stated annual goals will be measured and how that progress will be reported to the parents. Progress toward a goal is most often measured by using the short-term objectives, although formal assessment instruments are sometimes used. Especially in the general or inclusive physical education setting, paraeducators play an important role in helping the teacher determine progress toward annual goals by recording performance on a student's individual objectives. Because you are directly involved with the student, you can assist the physical educator in providing important feedback so that the IEP is revised appropriately and continues to meet the student's unique needs.

Paraeducator's Role in IEP Development and Implementation

Since paraeducators work on more of an individual basis with students with disabilities, they play a

▶ Paraeducators can assist the teachers by brainstorming ideas of game and activity modification so that the students can achieve their goals.

critical role in helping the students work on their IEP goals and short-term instructional objectives. The paraeducator can assist the general and adapted physical education teacher in three major areas: developing the IEP, implementing or infusing a student's goals and objectives into daily lessons and activities, and facilitating positive interactions among students. However, the physical education class is an active rather than sedentary classroom environment; therefore, expectations of the paraeducator are different.

In physical education, teachers are challenged with teaching groups of students with a wide range of levels in cognitive ability, behavior, and movement ability. This is true in both a separate adapted physical education class and a general physical education class. A general physical education class frequently contains several students with disabilities, each with different goals and objectives. This makes it difficult for the teacher to work on the goals of the entire class yet also assess and implement the different goals and objectives of students with disabilities within the class. Just like in Javier's class, in large classes it becomes extremely difficult for the physical educator to meet the instructional needs of both groups plus facilitate positive social interactions (Reams, 1997).

How to Assist With the PLP

A paraeducator can assist the physical educator by collecting data on student performance for the PLP as instructed. There are several ways to assist the physical educator in collecting assessment data so that an accurate description of a student's strengths and weaknesses is developed. For example, Javier's paraeducator may record the distance Javier jumps, his archery score, the number of times he throws a ball and hits a target, the number of times he strikes a ball, and so on.

A paraeducator can also assist with the development of the PLP by providing valuable input to the physical educator. For example, when Javier's

▶ Another role of paraeducators is to assist with assessment data by recording students' scores.

paraeducator shared her observations of Javier's behavior, reactions, and performance, it created a more complete picture of Javier's PLP. More importantly, you can play a critical role regarding the student's IEP goals and objectives. You can assist your student in this process by considering and taking action with the following information.

How to Assist With Short-Term Objectives

Helping to collect assessment data regarding student performance on short-term instructional objectives is a way for paraeducators to actively help the teacher with the IEP. As described in chapter 6, there are several ways the paraeducator can help the teacher determine if a student is making progress toward the annual goals and objectives, such as assisting with rubrics and checklists or gathering items for a student's portfolio.

Another way to help the teacher determine if a student is making progress toward annual goals is by recording performance on a student's individual short-term instructional objectives. For example, at a throwing station a student might increase the ability to hit a target with a tennis ball from 2 out of 10 to 8 out of 10 attempts. Javier's paraeducator keeps a chart of the number of times he is able to hit the center of the target from 6 feet (2 meters) away. The data will help the teacher determine if the student is making progress on the goal to improve throwing accuracy.

There are other ways you can serve an important role in the IEP process.

- Attend the IEP or parent–teacher meeting. Because paraeducators work more closely with the student with a disability, they often have different perceptions of the student than the teacher. You may be asked to assist the general or adapted physical educator in reporting on a student's progress during the IEP meeting or parent–teacher conference. For example, because Javier's paraeducator works closely with him, she can assist the teacher in reporting progress on IEP goals and objectives by sharing Javier's specific accomplishments with his parents on a regular basis.

- Sometimes, when the teacher is unable to attend the IEP meeting, you may be asked to attend and give the report in place of the teacher. In this case, you are not expected to write or give your own report. That is the teacher's role. You should be given a written report signed by the general or adapted physical educator that you bring to the IEP meeting and read in the place of the teacher. Because you know the student with a disability, your presence is important to provide clarification and examples and to answer any questions. It's much more helpful than someone simply reading the report!

How to Assist With Implementing Goals and Objectives Into Daily Lessons and Activities

One of the most important ways you can provide valuable educational services to students with disabilities is through implementing students' goals and objectives into daily lessons and activities. Here are some ways you can benefit your student.

- Know and understand your student's areas of strengths and weaknesses specific to physical education described in the PLP and the individual goals and objectives before you enter the gymnasium. When you understand these things, you can better help your student work on the areas that need improvement in each activity. Sometimes terminology and concepts in the PLP can be confusing. If you don't understand something, the physical education teacher, physical therapist, or occupational therapist can help.

- Facilitate the learning environment for your student. When paraeducators know a student's strengths and weaknesses, they can initiate minor changes to increase participation and improve the opportunity to learn during various activities. For example, if you know that your student hears better on the left side, does better with a weighted ball, is particularly chatty, or is distracted by certain stimuli, you can change the equipment or position in the group to help the student participate better (Daggett, 2004).

- Find out units of instruction and activity plans for the week before entering the gymnasium so that you can be ready to help your student work on the goals and short-term objectives.

Discuss with the teacher ahead of time how you can reinforce a student's goals and short-term objectives in the activities. For example, every other week Javier's paraeducator meets with the physical education teacher outside of class to talk about how Javier's goals and objectives can be worked into the upcoming units and activities.

- Carry out activities designed by the teacher to meet a student's short-term instructional objectives. For example, you may be asked to supervise and help your student practice skills with partners, in small groups, at stations, in circuits, and the like.

▶ By modeling proper form, paraeducators can help students practice skills, which is part of a paraeducator's job to help implement goals and objectives into the students' daily lessons and activities.

- Assist the teacher with making modifications and adjustments to existing units, lesson plans, and activities in order to connect them more directly to your student's short-term objectives. Modifying activities can include things like adding or changing equipment, adding or changing a task, or changing the distance or path. For example, let's say the physical education teacher has set up a variety of stations involving dribbling, catching, and throwing. At the throwing station Javier's paraeducator might suggest adding tennis balls and putting up targets of various sizes because one of Javier's short-term objectives is throwing a tennis ball at a 3- × 3-foot (1- × 1-meter) target from 6 feet (2 meters) away. Modifications and additions such as these not only help your student but also benefit the entire class.

- Share ideas for creating new or different activities. Teachers are constantly looking for new activities and games or variations on existing games. Because you understand your student's goals and needs, you may have ideas for a new activity or variation of a game that would help your student. Creative ideas not only can help your student but can be fun and beneficial for the entire class.

- Assist in facilitating socialization and positive interactions. Although the tendency is to protect students with a disability, it is important to keep socialization in mind during large-group activities. Avoid being too quick to step in and be your student's partner. Instead, seek out and encourage general education students to work together with your student. For example, if the class is working on basketball skills (bounce pass) and everyone in the class but your student has a partner, rather than being your student's partner, you could encourage a group of three to work on the skills together. As much as possible, try to work on your student's goals and objectives through a partner or group activity rather than working with the student on the side by yourself. This encourages interaction and increases

the possibility that students will continue the activity when you are not present.

- Share your student's accomplishments with parents on a regular basis. Because you are involved in recording data for IEPs, you can help parents understand their child's goals, performance, and progress.

Improving Social Behaviors

Teachers and paraeducators can create an environment within the classroom that is conducive to natural socialization. However, socialization is often difficult when students with disabilities exhibit undesirable and sometimes socially unacceptable behaviors. These behaviors may include one or more of the following: self-stimulating

▶ By sharing in the responsibility of improving the students' social skills, paraeducators help the students reduce any feelings of seclusion by helping the students develop relationships with each other.

behaviors (e.g., vocal sounds, twirling of the fingers, finger flicking, spinning), self-destructive behaviors (e.g., head banging, pinching, biting oneself), and aggressive behaviors toward others (e.g., kicking, hitting, biting, pulling hair, pinching).

Teachers and paraeducators share the responsibility for improving social skills of students with disabilities. There are many opportunities throughout the school day to teach and reinforce appropriate social behaviors. However, one of the best settings is the physical education class where peers, paraeducators, and teachers have the opportunity for socializing and interacting with students with disabilities. Because you have the greatest contact with the student throughout the school day, you can play a significant role in encouraging and reinforcing appropriate social behavior. By assisting in developing friendships and planning for and supporting social interactions, you can be instrumental in shaping social behaviors of students with disabilities. By helping peers develop friendships and supportive relationships with students with disabilities, you can help diminish the isolation that is often experienced and not understood by students with disabilities.

You can use two general strategies in helping your student develop and maintain appropriate social behaviors. The first strategy is to follow the same routine within a social setting. Occasional changes in a class structure or routine are allowable; however, sudden change can cause some students with disabilities to exhibit inappropriate behaviors (Block, 2007; Reid and O'Connor, 2003). The second strategy is to establish set cues and consequences as a positive management tool for teachers in order to change behaviors (Sherrill, 2004). With the physical educator and classroom teacher, you can help select specific cues or prompts in anticipation of inappropriate behavior, along with determining specific consequences in response to the behavior. When everyone uses consistent cues and consequences, students with disabilities who demonstrate inappropriate social behavior can be encouraged to redirect those behaviors.

Table 7.1 suggests additional ways paraeducators can encourage appropriate social behaviors and diminish inappropriate behaviors when working with students with disabilities.

▶ **TABLE 7.1 Dos and Don'ts for Teachers and Paraeducators to Encourage Positive Social Behaviors**

Dos	Don'ts
• Exhibit leadership. • Know all learners with and without disabilities. • Provide appropriate classroom arrangements that foster positive socialization. • Encourage age-appropriate behaviors and reinforce appropriate behaviors. • Pay attention to all learners. • Work with all learners (with and without disabilities) to increase motor and fitness skills. (For learners with disabilities, both pullout and inclusion settings may be appropriate.) • Find ways for learners with disabilities to be accepted. • Write objectives to improve social behaviors. • Record social behaviors to document progress. • Teach paraeducators how to record social behaviors. • Dispel misconceptions about learners' disabilities (e.g., not contagious). • Help peers to have equal-status relationships. • Encourage social interactions among all learners. • Help learners develop and maintain friendships. • Learn how to record social behaviors.	• Don't isolate learners with disabilities from the rest of the class. • Don't be negative toward learners with unacceptable behaviors. • Don't ignore social opportunities to develop peer interactions. • Don't rely too much on technology to help learners deal with social problems. • Don't hinder learners with disabilities from being self-sufficient and independent (know when to let go).

Sharing Information With Parents

Parents of children with disabilities are no different from parents whose children do not have disabilities: They want the best for their children. With ever-increasing time constraints, the physical education teacher may ask you to assist in communicating with parents. As the paraeducator, you are in a good position to work with parents because you know the child better than other school personnel do. Because you are involved in all aspects of the student's IEP, you can share goals and accomplishments with parents on a regular basis. This sharing helps parents understand their child's physical education program and develop more reasonable expectations for their child. When parents are informed about and involved in their children's physical activities, they are better able to become advocates of their children's educational programs (Karnes & Esry, 1981).

It is important to note that the new law (PL 108-446) states that if an area is discussed that includes a specific professional, then that professional must attend the meeting. This means that if the paraeducator is involved in physical education and it is being discussed at the IEP meeting, the paraeducator must attend. Paraeducators may be excused from such meetings only under parental consent. They may still be asked to submit written input.

You can also assist the teacher in helping parents learn some basic teaching and behavior management strategies and how to teach their children to play. In turn, parents can share information about what reinforcers tend to work with their children. Other ways you can help include teaching parents to make simple equipment that they can use at home and helping them identify and use community resources that are available to them.

Paraeducator's Role in Transition Programs

Students with disabilities typically develop their physical education skills in the classroom and practice them in the community. In order to best meet their transition goals and objectives, they also need both assistance and instruction at community-based recreation and leisure sites. The paraeducator plays an important role in providing students with the opportunity to work on their transitional objectives in the community. The paraeducator can accompany students to an off-campus site to practice recreational skills and reinforce what they learned in class. This does not necessarily mean that you are their partner; rather, you may facilitate participation and interaction in age-appropriate activities with their peers. This can be done in a variety of ways. The following are just a few suggestions:

- During physical education class, bicycle or roller-skate with them on the blacktop or around the school grounds.
- After school and during weekend programs, accompany and assist them in playing basketball, Ping-Pong, and so on at a local facility or at home.
- Accompany students into the community, such as going to a local fitness club or pool.

Many physical education teachers take learners aged 16 to 21 years to community events for

---

COMMUNITY-BASED PROGRAMMING RELATED TO THE IEP

Individual transition programs (ITP): Federal law (IDEA) now requires a different type of IEP for adolescents. Once students reach the age of 14, the focus of the IEP shifts from school-based programs to helping students successfully transition into the community when they graduate from high school (Auxter et al., 2005; Short, 2005). In every content area, transition goals and short-term objectives target activities and life skills in the community including employment, independent living, and recreation and leisure. Teaching students to participate in age-appropriate recreational activities (both group and individual) can be important in helping students with disabilities successfully transition into the community (Demchak, 1994). In physical education, there are many individual and team recreational and leisure activities that students with disabilities can participate in when they are in the community. These include roller, ice, and in-line skating; basketball; swimming; horseback riding; rock climbing; bowling; bicycling; kayaking; weight training; step aerobics; and so on (Modell & Megginson, 2001). This list is endless and should be based on the student's needs, desires, and capabilities.

---

transition activities in physical education. As the paraeducator, you play an extremely important part in these experiences outside of school by accompanying your student.

For students to fully realize their physical education goals, they must successfully transition into the community and develop a healthy, independent lifestyle. Ultimately, we want to empower the students to access health-related fitness, physical activity, and sport activities on their own, facilitating their social interaction, friendships, family recreation, community participation, and positive use of leisure time.

Parents often ask the teacher what community-based opportunities are available for their child. Because you are in contact with parents as well as teachers, you can help provide the necessary information. Your knowledge of what opportunities exist in the community and your assistance in going to various events are invaluable. A directory of available opportunities could be given to parents either by e-mail or hard copy. Generally students with a disability can participate in the same or similar physical activities as their same-age peers (Block, 2007). Many community-based programs are integrated, meaning that children with and without disabilities participate together. If the child with a disability cannot participate meaningfully in an integrated program, an alternative program should be offered.

One of the best-known community programs is Special Olympics, which provides athletic competition for individuals with intellectual disabilities. In addition, Special Olympics has an integrated component, Unified Sports, in which half the participants have intellectual disabilities and the other half do not have a disability. Although the Special Olympics sport skills manuals contain a great deal of information about competition, the primary emphasis is providing opportunities to learn and use the skills in the community. The Motor Activities Training Program (MATP) of Special Olympics serves individuals with severe intellectual disabilities with activities that are functional (skills deemed important and suitable for people with severe disabilities). These activities and the sports they lead into are mobility (gymnastics), dexterity (athletics, or track and field), striking (softball), kicking (soccer), manual wheelchair (athletics), motorized wheelchair (athletics), and aquatics. The best way to acquire information about local Special Olympics is to find out what is being offered in the home community. Each state has a Web site that gives contact information for the various areas.

There are other programs that offer alternative community programs in many sports, such as the Paralympics. The USA Deaf Sports Federation (USADSF) provides sport opportunities to individuals who are deaf. The National Disability Sports Alliance (NDSA) provides opportunities in sport for people with cerebral palsy, traumatic brain injury, and stroke. Wheelchair Sports, USA provides a number of sports for athletes who use wheelchairs, especially wheelchair basketball and wheelchair tennis. Disabled Sports USA (DS/USA) provides opportunities in winter sports and water, recreational, and fitness activities. The Dwarf Athletic Association of America (DAAA) offers sport opportunities for individuals who are dwarfs. The United States Association of Blind Athletes (USABA) offers sport opportunities for people with visual impairments and blindness.

Summary

More than ever, paraeducators are relied upon to assist with the education of students with disabilities in the general physical education setting. Although there are many responsibilities, none is as important as facilitating the development and implementation of a student's IEP. As a result of reading this chapter, you now know the various components of the IEP and how you can assist in the IEP process. More importantly, you now understand the valuable role the paraeducator serves in the implementation of the IEP. In addition, this chapter discussed how you can assist with implementing transition programs into the community for high school students, educating parents, and improving appropriate social behaviors of students with disabilities. As the paraeducator, you play a vital role assisting the physical educator in every aspect of the IEP process for students of all ages, from referral to transition programs.

Paraeducator Responsibilities

The following is a sample job description for an adapted physical education paraeducator.

General Job Description

Work with students who require more individualized attention during the physical education lesson.

Specific Job Description

The following are specific duties to be carried out by the paraeducator:

1. Establish a positive and supportive relationship with the physical education teacher through regular meetings and communication.

2. Work with individuals or groups of students under the direct supervision of the physical education teacher.

3. Assist with activities of the daily lesson by

   - demonstrating or having another student correctly demonstrate the skill or activity under instruction;

   - closely supervising students in teacher-planned activities, including physically standing an arm's-reach away as needed;

   - helping students stay on task for activities taught by the physical education teacher through motivation, assistance, and the like;

   - using appropriate activity modifications of equipment, rules, and so on, as approved by the physical education teacher;

   - allowing students to perform skills and activities as independently as possible; and

   - facilitating positive, age-appropriate interaction between the students and their peers.

4. Implement approved behavior management program for students in the gymnasium consistent with the plan used in the classroom.

5. Assess students' skill and activity performances as requested by the physical education teacher.

6. Record progress of students under the direction of the physical education teacher.

7. Prepare and obtain instructional materials (e.g., equipment, written instructions) as needed for the lesson's activities in consultation with the physical education teacher.

8. Accompany students during any community experiences.

9. Assist students with toileting, dressing, and other self-care activities when needed.

10. Uphold confidentiality guidelines pertaining to students, parents, and physical education activities. All parent communication must come from the certified physical education teacher.

11. Perform other duties as assigned by the physical education teacher.

National Dissemination Center for Children with Disabilities (NICHCY) Disability Fact Sheets

The following list contains information about specific disabilities taken from the *National Dissemination Center for Children with Disabilities* (NICHCY) Disability Fact Sheets. The more you know about a child and the disability, the more prepared you will be to meet all unique needs. More information about these disabilities and others can be found on their Web site at www.nichcy.org.

Autism and Pervasive Developmental Disorder

Definition

Autism and pervasive developmental disorder, not otherwise specified (PDD-NOS) are developmental disabilities that share many of the same characteristics. Usually evident by age 3, autism and PDD-NOS are neurological disorders that affect a child's ability to communicate, understand language, play, and relate to others.

In the diagnostic manual used to classify disabilities, the *Diagnostic and Statistical Manual of Mental Disorders, Fourth Edition* (DSM IV), autistic disorder is listed under the heading of pervasive developmental disorders. A diagnosis of autistic disorder is made when a person displays 6 or more of 12 symptoms listed across three major areas: social interaction, communication, and behavior. When children display similar behaviors but do not meet the criteria for autistic disorder, they may receive a diagnosis of PDD-

NOS. Although the diagnosis is called PDD-NOS, throughout the remainder of this fact sheet, we will refer to the diagnosis as PDD because this designation is more commonly known.

Autistic disorder is one of the disabilities specifically defined in IDEA, the federal legislation under which young people with disabilities receive special education and related services. IDEA (1997), which uses the term autism, defines the disorder as "a developmental disability significantly affecting verbal and nonverbal communication and social interaction, usually evident before age 3, that adversely affects a child's educational performance. Other characteristics often associated with autism are engagement in repetitive activities and stereotyped movements, resistance to environmental change or change in daily routines, and unusual responses to sensory experiences." In keeping with IDEA and the way in which this disorder is generally referred to in the field, we will use the term autism throughout the remainder of this fact sheet.

Due to the similarity of behaviors associated with autism and PDD, use of the term pervasive developmental disorder has caused some confusion among parents and professionals. However, the treatment and educational needs are similar for both diagnoses.

Characteristics

Some or all of the following characteristics may be observed in mild to severe forms: communication problems (e.g., using and understanding language); difficulty relating to people, objects, and events; unusual play with toys and other objects; difficulty with changes in routine or familiar surroundings; and repetitive body movements or behavior patterns.

Children with autism or PDD vary widely in abilities, intelligence, and behavior. Some children do not speak; others have limited language skills that often include repeated phrases or conversations. People with more advanced language skills tend to focus on a small range of topics and have difficulty with abstract concepts. Repetitive play skills, a limited range of interests, and impaired social skills are generally evident as well. Unusual responses to sensory information—for example, loud noises, lights, certain textures of food or fabrics—are also common.

Educational Implications

Early diagnosis and appropriate educational programs are very important to children with autism or PDD. IDEA includes autism as a disability category. From the age of 3, children with autism and PDD are eligible for an educational program appropriate to their individual needs. Educational programs for students with autism or PDD focus on improving communication and social, academic, behavioral, and daily living skills. Behavior and communication problems that interfere with learning sometimes require the assistance of a knowledgeable professional in the autism field who develops and helps implement a plan that can be carried out at home and school.

The classroom environment should be structured so that the program is consistent and predictable. Students with autism or PDD learn better and are less confused when information is presented visually as well as verbally. Interaction with peers without disabilities is also important because these students provide models of appropriate language, social, and behavioral skills. To overcome frequent problems in generalizing (transferring) skills learned at school, it is important to develop programs with parents so that learning activities, experiences, and approaches can be carried over into the home and community.

With educational programs designed to meet a student's individual needs and specialized adult support services in employment and living arrangements, children and adults with autism or PDD can live and work in the community.

Tips for Paraeducators

The following are a few tips for paraeducators when working with students with autism and PDD.

- Communicate and collaborate with the physical education teacher to implement the student's IEP goals.
- Use the same behavior modification program in the gym as in the classroom.
- Work with the student in a less stimulating area of the gym. Use mats to make the student a small room within the gym if necessary.
- Prepare the student to transition in and out of the gym environment and between activities through picture cards, words, sign language, or other means.
- Use a set or predictable routine.
- Be consistent in use of terms, equipment, and sequence of activities.
- Use moderate aerobic exercise to reduce self-stimulating behavior.
- Use repetitive activities such as roller-skating or bicycle riding.
- Demonstrate activities for the student to imitate.
- Work one on one with the student or in groups no larger than three.
- Encourage the student to communicate with words.

Organizations

Autism National Committee (ANC)
P.O. Box 429
Forest Knolls, CA 94933
www.autcom.org

Autism Services Center (ASC)
P.O. Box 507
Huntington, WV 25710-0507
304-525-8014
www.autismservicescenter.org

Autism Society of America (ASA)
7910 Woodmont Ave., Ste. 300
Bethesda, MD 20814
800-328-8476
301-657-0881
info@autism-society.org
www.autism-society.org

Indiana Resource Center for Autism (IRCA)
Indiana Institute on Disability and Community
2853 East 10th St., Indiana University
Bloomington, IN 47408-2696
812-855-6508 (voice)
812-855-9396 (TTY)
www.iidc.indiana.edu/irca

Cerebral Palsy

Definition

Cerebral palsy, also known as *CP*, is a condition caused by injury to the parts of the brain that control the muscles. *Cerebral* means having to do with the brain, and *palsy* refers to weakness or problems with using the muscles. Often the injury happens before birth, but sometimes it occurs during delivery or soon after being born. CP can be mild, moderate, or severe. Mild CP may mean a child is clumsy, moderate CP may mean the child walks with a limp and may need a special leg brace or a cane, and severe CP may affect all parts of a child's physical abilities. A child with moderate or severe CP may have to use a wheelchair and other special equipment. Sometimes children with CP also have learning problems, problems with hearing or seeing (called *sensory problems*), or an intellectual disability. Usually, the greater the injury to the brain, the more severe the CP; however, CP doesn't worsen over time, and most children with CP have a normal life span.

CP as an Orthopedic Impairment

IDEA guides how early intervention services and special education and related services are provided to children with disabilities. Under IDEA (1997), CP is considered an orthopedic impairment, which is defined as "a severe orthopedic impairment that adversely affects a child's educational performance. The term includes impairments caused by congenital anomaly (e.g., clubfoot, absence of some member, etc.), impairments caused by disease (e.g., poliomyelitis, bone tuberculosis, etc.), and impairments from other causes (e.g., cerebral palsy, amputations, and fractures or burns that cause contractures)."

Characteristics

There are three main types of CP.

- *Spastic CP* is where there is too much muscle tone or tightness. Movements are stiff, especially in the legs, arms, and back. Children with this form of CP move their legs awkwardly, turning in or scissoring their legs as they walk. This is the most common form of CP.

- *Athetoid CP* (also called *dyskinetic CP*) can affect movements of the entire body. Typically, this form of CP involves slow, uncontrolled body movements and low muscle tone that makes it difficult to sit up straight and to walk.

- *Mixed CP* is a combination of the symptoms listed previously. A child with mixed CP has both high and low muscle tone. This means that some muscles are too tight and others are too loose, creating a mix of stiffness and involuntary movements. More terms used to describe the different types of CP include the following:

  - *Diplegia* indicates that only the legs are affected.

  - *Hemiplegia* indicates that one-half of the body (such as the right arm and leg) is affected.

  - *Quadriplegia* indicates that both arms and legs are affected, and sometimes the facial muscles and torso as well.

Treatment

Early and ongoing treatment can reduce the effects of CP. Many children learn how to make their bodies work for them in other ways. For example, an infant who is unable to crawl may be able to get around by rolling from place to place.

Children younger than 3 years old can benefit greatly from early intervention. Early intervention is a system of services to support infants and toddlers with disabilities and their families. For older children, special education and related services are available through public school to help each child achieve and learn.

Children with CP may need different kinds of therapy, including the following:

- *Physical therapy* (PT), which helps the child develop stronger muscles such as those in the legs and trunk. Through PT, the child works on skills such as walking, sitting, and maintaining balance.

- *Occupational therapy* (OT), which helps the child develop fine motor skills used in daily living, such as dressing, feeding, writing, and so on.
- *Speech-language pathology* (S/L), which helps the child develop communication skills. The child may work in particular on speaking, which may be difficult due to problems with muscle tone of the tongue and throat.

Children with CP may also find a variety of special equipment helpful. For example, braces (also called *ankle–foot orthoses,* or AFOs) may be used to hold the feet in place when the child stands or walks. Custom splints can provide support to help children use their hands. In addition, a variety of therapy equipment and adapted toys are available to help children play and have fun while they are working their bodies. Activities such as swimming or horseback riding can also help strengthen weaker muscles and relax tighter ones.

New medical treatments are being developed all the time. Sometimes surgery, Botox injections, or other medications can help lessen the effects of CP, but there is no cure.

Educational Implications

A child with CP can face many challenges in school and is likely to need individualized attention. Fortunately, states are responsible for meeting the educational needs of children with disabilities. For children up to the age of 3, services are provided through an early intervention system. School staff members work with the child's family to develop an IFSP (see chapter 7). The plan describes the child's unique needs as well as the services the child will receive to address those needs. The IFSP also emphasizes the unique needs of the family so that parents and other family members will know how to help their child with CP. Early intervention services may be provided on a sliding-fee basis, meaning that the costs to the family will depend upon their income.

For school-aged children, including preschoolers, special education and related services are provided through the school system. School staff members work with the child's parents to develop an IEP (see chapter 7). The IEP is similar to the IFSP in that it describes the child's unique needs and the services that have been designed to meet those needs. Special education and related services, which can include PT, OT, and S/L, are provided at no cost to parents.

In addition to therapy services and special equipment, children with CP may need what is known as *assistive technology.* Examples of assistive technology include the following.

- *Communication devices* can range from simple to sophisticated. Communication boards, for example, have pictures, symbols, letters, or words attached. The child communicates by pointing to or gazing at the pictures or symbols. Augmentative communication devices are more sophisticated and include voice synthesizers that enable the child to talk with others.
- *Computer technology* can range from electronic toys with special switches to sophisticated computer programs operated by simple switch pads or keyboard adaptations.

The ability of the brain to find new ways of working after an injury is remarkable. Even so, it can be difficult for parents to imagine what their child's future will be like. Good therapy and handling can help, but the most important treatment the child can receive is love and encouragement along with lots of typical childhood experiences with family and friends. With the right mix of support, equipment, extra time, and accommodations, all children with CP can be successful learners and full participants in life.

Tips for Paraeducators

The following are a few tips for paraeducators when working with students with CP.

- Learn more about CP. The resources and organizations listed at the end of this section will help you.
- Sometimes the appearance of CP can give the mistaken impression that a child who has CP cannot learn as much as others. Focus on the individual and learn firsthand what needs and capabilities the child has.
- Tap into the strategies that teachers use for students with learning disabilities. Become

knowledgeable about different learning styles. Then you can use the approach best suited for a particular child based upon that child's learning abilities as well as physical abilities.

- Be inventive. Ask yourself (and others), "How can I adapt this lesson for this child to maximize active, hands-on learning?"

- Learn to love assistive technology. Find experts within and outside your school to help you. Assistive technology can mean the difference between independence and dependence for your student.

- Always remember, parents are experts, too. Talk candidly with your student's parents. They can tell you a great deal about their child's special needs and abilities.

- Effective teamwork for the child with CP needs to bring together professionals with diverse backgrounds and expertise. The team must combine the knowledge of its members to plan, implement, and coordinate the child's services.

- Communicate and collaborate with the physical education teacher to implement the student's IEP goals.

- Work on muscle stretching, especially for students with spastic CP.

- Develop the student's range of motion.

- Develop postural alignments through muscle stretching and strengthening.

- If the student can walk, use ramp climbing and develop gait training.

- Use hand-over-hand activities when necessary to help the student perform a task.

- Use switches to help the student perform activities in the gymnasium.

- Use adapted equipment to help the student perform movement tasks, such as a bowling-ball ramp to push a ball.

- Lift the body or body parts against gravity to develop muscle strength.

Organizations

Easter Seals National Office
230 W. Monroe St., Ste. 1800
Chicago, IL 60606-4802
800-221-6827 (voice)

312-726-6200 (voice)
312-726-4258 (TTY)
www.easter-seals.org

United Cerebral Palsy (UCP)
1660 L St. NW, Ste. 700
Washington, DC 20036
800-872-5827 (voice, TTY)
202-776-0406 (voice)
202-973-7197 (TTY)
www.ucp.org

Deafness and Hearing Loss

Definition

IDEA includes hearing impairment and deafness as two of the categories under which children with disabilities may be eligible for special education and related services programming. While the term *hearing impairment* is often used to describe a wide range of hearing losses, including deafness, IDEA defines hearing loss and deafness separately.

Hearing impairment is defined by IDEA (1997) as "an impairment in hearing, whether permanent or fluctuating, that adversely affects a child's educational performance."

Deafness is defined as "a hearing impairment that is so severe that the child is impaired in processing linguistic information through hearing, with or without amplification."

Thus, deafness may be viewed as a condition that prevents a person from receiving sound in all or most of its forms. In contrast, a child with a hearing loss can generally respond to auditory stimuli, including speech.

Characteristics

It is useful to know that sound is measured by its loudness or intensity (in units called *decibels,* or dB) and its frequency or pitch (in units called *hertz,* or Hz). Impairment can occur in either or both areas, and it may exist in only one ear or in both ears. Hearing loss is generally described as slight, mild, moderate, severe, or profound, depending on how well a person can hear the intensities or frequencies most greatly associated with speech. Generally, only children whose hearing loss is greater than 90 dB are considered deaf for the purposes of educational placement.

There are four types of hearing loss. *Conductive hearing losses* are caused by diseases or obstructions in the outer or middle ear (the conduction pathways for sound to reach the inner ear). Conductive hearing losses usually affect all frequencies of hearing evenly and do not result in severe losses. A person with a conductive hearing loss usually is able to use a hearing aid or can be helped medically or surgically.

Sensorineural hearing losses result from damage to the delicate sensory hair cells of the inner ear or the nerves that supply the inner ear. These hearing losses can range from mild to profound and often affect the person's ability to hear specific frequencies. Thus, even with amplification to increase the sound level, a person with a sensorineural hearing loss may perceive distorted sounds, sometimes making the use of a hearing aid impossible.

Mixed hearing losses are a combination of conductive and sensorineural losses, which means that a problem occurs in both the outer or middle ear and the inner ear. Finally, *central hearing losses* result from damage or impairment to the nerves or nuclei of the central nervous system, either in the pathways to the brain or in the brain itself.

Educational Implications

Hearing loss or deafness does not affect a person's intellectual capacity or ability to learn. However, children who are either hard of hearing or deaf generally require special education services in order to receive an adequate education. Such services may include the following.

- Regular speech, language, and auditory training from a specialist
- Amplification systems
- Interpreter services for students who use sign language
- Favorable seating in the class to facilitate lip reading
- Captioned films and videos
- Assistance of a note-taker, who takes notes so that the student can fully attend to instruction

- Instruction for the teacher and peers in alternate communication methods, such as sign language
- Counseling

Children who are hard of hearing will find it much more difficult than children who have normal hearing to learn vocabulary, grammar, word order, idiomatic expressions, and other aspects of verbal communication. For children who are deaf or have severe hearing losses, early, consistent, and conscious use of visible communication modes (such as sign language, finger spelling, and Cued Speech) or amplification and aural and oral training can help reduce this language delay. By age 4 or 5, most children who are deaf are enrolled in school full time and do special work on communication and language development. It is important for teachers and audiologists to work together to teach children to use their residual hearing to the maximum extent possible, even if the preferred means of communication is manual. Since the majority of deaf children (more than 90%) are born to hearing parents, programs should provide instruction for parents on the implications of deafness within the family.

People with hearing loss use oral or manual means of communication or a combination of both. Oral communication includes speech, lip reading, and the use of residual hearing. Manual communication involves signs and finger spelling. Total Communication is a method of instruction that combines the oral method plus signing and finger spelling.

Many helpful devices are now available to people with hearing loss, including those who are deaf. Text telephones (known as TTs, TTYs, or TDDs) enable people to type phone messages over the telephone network. The Telecommunications Relay Service (TRS), now required by law, makes it possible for TTY users to communicate with virtually anyone via telephone. Dial 7-1-1 to access TRS for free anywhere in the United States.

Tips for Paraeducators

The following are a few tips for paraeducators when working with students with deafness or who are hard of hearing.

- Communicate and collaborate with the physical education teacher to implement the student's IEP goals.

- Stand close to the student when communicating.
- Face the student when you talk, making sure the student can see your lips.
- Visually demonstrate each skill the student is learning.
- Use the same communication method in the gym as in the classroom.
- Learn basic signs that will be used in the gym, such as *ball, go,* and *stop,* and use them consistently.
- Stand still when giving instructions.
- Write down instructions or information if necessary.
- Develop and use a consistent signal to gain the student's attention when playing a game.

Organizations

Alexander Graham Bell Association
  for the Deaf and Hard of Hearing
3417 Volta Place, NW
Washington, DC 20007
202-337-5220 (voice)
202-337-5221 (TTY)
info@agbell.org
www.agbell.org

American Society for Deaf Children (ASDC)
3820 Hartzdale Dr.
Camp Hill, PA 17011
800-942-2732 (voice, TTY)
717-909-5599 (voice, TTY)
asdc@deafchildren.org
www.deafchildren.org

American Speech-Language-Hearing
  Association (ASHA)
10801 Rockville Pike
Rockville, MD 20852
301-897-5700 (voice, TTY)
800-638-8255 (voice, TTY)
www.asha.org

Laurent Clerc National Deaf Education Center
KDES PAS-6, Gallaudet University
800 Florida Ave. NE
Washington, DC 20002-3695
202-651-5051 (voice, TTY)
http://clerccenter.gallaudet.edu/InfoToGo/
  index.html

Down Syndrome

Definition

Down syndrome is the most common and readily identifiable chromosomal condition associated with an intellectual disability. For some unexplained reason, an accident in cell development results in 47 chromosomes instead of the usual 46. This extra chromosome changes the orderly development of the body and brain. In most cases, Down syndrome is diagnosed according to results from a chromosome test administered shortly after birth.

Characteristics

There are more than 50 clinical signs of Down syndrome, but it is rare to find all or even most of them in one person. Some common characteristics include the following:

- Poor muscle tone
- Slanting eyes with folds of skin at the inner corners (called *epicanthal folds)*
- Hyperflexibility (excessive ability to extend the joints)
- Short, broad hands with a single crease across the palm on one or both hands
- Broad feet with short toes
- Flat bridge of the nose
- Short, low-set ears
- Short neck
- Small head
- Small oral cavity
- Short, high-pitched cries in infancy

Individuals with Down syndrome are usually smaller than their peers without Down syndrome, and their physical as well as intellectual development is slower.

Besides having a distinct physical appearance, children with Down syndrome frequently have specific health problems. A lowered resistance to infection makes them more prone to respiratory problems. Visual problems such as crossed eyes and far- or nearsightedness are higher in people with Down syndrome, as are mild to moderate hearing loss and speech difficulty.

Approximately one-third of babies born with Down syndrome have heart defects, most of which are now correctable. Some babies are born with gastrointestinal tract problems that can be surgically corrected.

Some people with Down syndrome also may have atlantoaxial instability, a misalignment of the top two vertebrae of the neck. This condition makes these individuals more prone to injury if they participate in activities that overextend or flex the neck. Parents are urged to have their child examined by a physician to determine whether their child should be restricted from sports and activities that place stress on the neck. Although this misalignment is a potentially serious condition, proper diagnosis can help prevent serious injury.

Children with Down syndrome have a tendency to become obese as they grow older. Besides having negative social implications, this weight gain threatens their health and longevity. A supervised diet and exercise program may help reduce this problem.

Educational Implications

Shortly after a diagnosis of Down syndrome is confirmed, parents should be encouraged to enroll their child in an early intervention program. These programs offer parents special instruction in teaching their child language, cognitive, self-help, and social skills, as well as specific exercises for gross and fine motor development. Research has shown that stimulation during early developmental stages improves children's chances of developing to their fullest potential. Continuing education, positive public attitudes, and a stimulating home environment have also been found to promote overall development.

Just as in the population without Down syndrome, there is a wide variation in mental abilities, behavior, and developmental progress in people with Down syndrome. Their level of intellectual disability may range from mild to severe, with the majority functioning in the mild to moderate range. Due to these individual differences, it is impossible to predict future achievements of children with Down syndrome.

Because of this range of ability, it is important for families and all members of the student's education team to place few limitations on potential capabilities. It may be effective to emphasize concrete concepts rather than abstract ideas. Teaching tasks in a step-by-step manner with frequent reinforcement and consistent feedback has been proven successful. Improved public acceptance of people with disabilities, along with increased opportunities for adults with disabilities to live and work independently in the community, has expanded goals for individuals with Down syndrome. Independent living centers, shared and supervised apartments, and support services in the community have proven to be important resources for people with Down syndrome.

Tips for Paraeducators

The following are a few tips for paraeducators when working with students with Down syndrome.

- Communicate and collaborate with the physical education teacher to implement the student's IEP goals.
- Break skills down into step-by-step instructions, demonstrating each step.
- Develop the student's muscle strength to compensate for low muscle tone.
- Repeat information and instructions often.
- Put the student in less demanding sport positions.
- Be consistent in use of terms, equipment, and sequence of activities.
- Work on the student's physical fitness.
- If the student has atlantoaxial instability, avoid activities that put pressure on the neck muscles, such as diving, gymnastics, and soccer.

Organizations

The Arc of the United States (formerly the Association for Retarded Citizens of the United States)
1010 Wayne Ave., Ste. 650
Silver Spring, MD 20910
301-565-3842
info@thearc.org
www.thearc.org

National Down Syndrome Congress (NDSC)
1370 Center Dr., Ste. 102
Atlanta, GA 30338

800-232-6372
770-604-9500
info@ndsccenter.org
www.ndsccenter.org

National Down Syndrome Society (NDSS)
666 Broadway
New York, NY 10012
800-221-4602
212-460-9330
info@ndss.org
www.ndss.org

Emotional Disturbance

Definition

Many terms are used to describe emotional, behavioral, or mental disorders. Currently, students with such disorders are categorized as having an *emotional disturbance,* which is defined under IDEA (1997) as "a condition exhibiting one or more of the following characteristics over a long period of time and to a marked degree that adversely affects a child's educational performance: a) an inability to learn that cannot be explained by intellectual, sensory, or health factors; b) an inability to build or maintain satisfactory interpersonal relationships with peers and teachers; c) inappropriate types of behavior or feelings under normal circumstances; d) a general pervasive mood of unhappiness or depression; e) a tendency to develop physical symptoms or fears associated with personal or school problems."

As defined by IDEA, emotional disturbance includes schizophrenia but does not apply to children who are socially maladjusted unless it is determined that they have an emotional disturbance.

Characteristics

The causes of emotional disturbance have not been adequately determined. Although various factors such as heredity, brain disorder, diet, stress, and family functioning have been suggested as possible causes, research has not shown any of these factors to be the direct cause of behavioral or emotional problems. Some of the characteristics and behaviors seen in children who have emotional disturbances include the following.

- Hyperactivity (short attention span, impulsiveness)
- Aggression or self-injurious behavior (acting out, fighting)
- Withdrawal (failure to initiate interaction with others, retreating from exchanges of social interaction, excessive fear or anxiety)
- Immaturity (inappropriate crying, temper tantrums, poor coping skills)
- Learning difficulties (performing below grade level)

Children with the most serious emotional disturbances may exhibit distorted thinking, excessive anxiety, bizarre motor acts, and abnormal mood swings. Some have severe psychosis or schizophrenia.

Many children who do not have emotional disturbances may display some of these same behaviors at various times during their development. However, when children have an emotional disturbance, these behaviors continue over long periods of time. Their behavior thus signals that they are not coping with their environment or peers.

Educational Implications

Educational programs for children with an emotional disturbance need to focus on providing emotional and behavioral support as well as helping them to master academics; develop social skills; and increase self-awareness, self-control, and self-esteem. A large body of research exists regarding methods of providing PBS in the school environment so that problem behaviors are minimized and positive behaviors are fostered (see chapter 4). It is also important to know the following:

- For a child whose behavior impedes learning (including the learning of others), the team developing the child's IEP needs to consider strategies to address that behavior, including positive behavioral interventions, strategies, and support.
- Students eligible for special education services under the category of emotional disturbance may have IEPs that include psychological or counseling services. These are important related services that are available under law and are to be provided by a social

worker, psychologist, guidance counselor, or other qualified personnel.

- Career education (both vocational and academic) is also a major part of secondary education and should be a part of the transition plan included in every adolescent's IEP.

There is growing recognition that families, as well as their children, need support; respite care; intensive case management; and a collaborative, multiagency approach to services. Many communities are working toward providing these services. A growing number of agencies and organizations are actively involved in establishing support services in the community.

Tips for Paraeducators

The following are a few tips for paraeducators when working with students with emotional disturbance.

- Communicate and collaborate with the physical education teacher to implement the student's IEP goals.
- Remove distracting objects from the gymnasium.
- Remove handheld weights and other objects from the gymnasium that could be thrown in anger.
- Play games that stress positive social interaction with peers.
- Expect aggressiveness but monitor it closely.
- Use activities that provide immediate, positive feedback.
- Help the student avoid inappropriate interaction with peers.
- Set appropriate behavior limits and consistently enforce them.
- Use the same behavior plan in the gym as in the classroom.

Organizations

American Academy of Child and Adolescent Psychiatry (AACAP)
Public Information Office
3615 Wisconsin Ave. NW
Washington, DC 20016-3007
202-966-7300
www.aacap.org

Federation of Families for Children's Mental Health (FFCMH)
9605 Medical Center Dr.
Rockville, MD 20850
240-403-1901
ffcmh@ffcmh.org

Mental Health America (MHA) (formerly National Mental Health Association)
2000 N. Beauregard St., 6th Floor
Alexandria, VA 22311
703-684-7722
800-969-6642
800-433-5959 (TTY)
www.nmha.org

National Mental Health Information Center (NMHC)
P.O. Box 42557
Washington, DC 20015
800-789-2647
www.mentalhealth.org

Learning Disabilities

Definition

Learning disability (LD) is a general term that describes specific kinds of learning problems. Such disabilities can cause a person to have trouble learning and using certain skills. The skills most often affected are reading, writing, listening, speaking, reasoning, and doing math.

IDEA (1997) defines an LD as "a disorder in one or more of the basic psychological processes involved in understanding or in using language, spoken or written, that may manifest itself in an imperfect ability to listen, think, speak, read, write, spell, or do mathematical calculations, including conditions such as perceptual disabilities, brain injury, minimal brain dysfunction, dyslexia, and developmental aphasia."

Such disabilities do not include "learning problems that are primarily the result of visual, hearing, or motor disabilities, of mental retardation, of emotional disturbance, or of environmental, cultural, or economic disadvantage."

Disabilities vary from person to person. For example, one person with LD may have trouble reading and writing, another person may have problems understanding math, and still another person may have trouble in each of these areas as well as with understanding what people are saying.

Researchers think that these disabilities are caused by differences in how a person's brain works and how it processes information. Children with such disabilities are not dumb or lazy; in fact, they usually have average or above-average intelligence. Their brains just process information differently.

There is no cure for these disabilities; they are lifelong. However, children with LD can be high achievers and can be taught ways to get around the disability. With the right help, children with LD can learn successfully.

Characteristics

There is no one sign that shows a person has LD. Experts look for a noticeable difference between how well children do in school and how well they could do given their intelligence or ability. There are also certain clues that may mean a child has LD. Most relate to elementary school tasks, because such disabilities tend to be identified in elementary school. A child probably won't show all of these signs, or even most of them. However, if a child shows a number of the following problems, then parents and the teacher should consider the possibility that the child has LD.

Children with LD

- may have trouble learning the alphabet, rhyming words, or connecting letters to their sounds;

- may make many mistakes when reading aloud, and repeat and pause often;

- may not understand what they read;

- may have trouble with spelling;

- may have very messy handwriting or hold a pencil awkwardly;

- may struggle to express ideas in writing;

- may learn language late and have a limited vocabulary;

- may have trouble remembering the sounds that letters make or hearing slight differences between words;

- may have trouble understanding jokes, comic strips, and sarcasm;

- may have trouble following directions;

- may mispronounce words or use a wrong word that sounds similar;

- may have trouble organizing what they want to say or not be able to think of the word they need for writing or conversation;

- may not follow the social rules of conversation, such as taking turns, and may stand too close to the listener;

- may confuse math symbols and misread numbers;

- may not be able to retell a story in order (i.e., what happened first, second, third); or

- may not know where to begin a task or how to go on from there.

If a child has unexpected problems learning to read, write, listen, speak, or do math, then teachers and parents may want to investigate more and have the child evaluated. The same is true if the child is struggling to do any one of these skills.

Educational Implications

LDs tend to be diagnosed when children reach school age. This is because school focuses on the very things that may be difficult for the child—reading, writing, math, listening, speaking, and reasoning. Teachers and parents notice that the child is not learning as expected. The school may ask to evaluate the child to see what is causing the problem. Parents can also ask for their child to be evaluated.

With hard work and the proper help, children with LD can learn more easily and successfully. For school-aged children (including preschoolers), special education and related services are important sources of help. School staff members work with the child's parents to develop an IEP that describes the child's unique needs and the special education services that will be provided to meet those needs. These services are provided at no cost to the child or family.

Supports or changes in the classroom (sometimes called *accommodations*) help most students with LD. Some common accommodations are listed later in Tips for Paraeducators. Assistive technology can also help many students work around their disabilities. Assistive technology can range from low-tech equipment such as tape recorders to high-tech tools such as reading machines (which read books aloud) and voice recognition systems (which allow the student to write by talking to the computer).

It's important to remember that a child may need help at home as well as in school. The resources listed at the end of the section will help families and teachers learn more about the many ways to help children with LD.

Tips for Paraeducators

The following are a few tips for paraeducators when working with students with LD.

- Learn as much as you can about the different types of LD. The resources and organizations at the end of this section can help you identify specific techniques and strategies to support the student.

- Seize the opportunity to make an enormous difference in this student's life. Find out and emphasize the student's strengths and interests. Give the student positive feedback and lots of opportunities for practice.

- Review the student's evaluation records to identify where specifically the student has trouble. Talk to specialists in your school (e.g., special educators) about methods for teaching this student. Provide instruction and accommodations to address the student's special needs. Examples include
    - breaking tasks into smaller steps and giving directions verbally and in writing;
    - giving the student more time to finish schoolwork or take tests;
    - letting the student with reading problems use audio versions of textbooks (available through Recording for the Blind and Dyslexic, listed under Organizations);
    - letting the student with listening difficulties borrow notes from a classmate or use a tape recorder; and
    - letting the student with writing difficulties use a computer with specialized software that spell checks, grammar checks, or recognizes speech.

- Learn about the different testing modifications that can help students with LD show what they have learned. Teach organizational skills, study skills, and learning strategies. These help all students but are particularly helpful for those with LD.

- Work with the student's parents to create an educational plan tailored to meet the student's needs.

- Establish a positive working relationship with the student's parents. Through regular communication, exchange information about the student's progress at school.

- Communicate and collaborate with the physical education teacher to implement the student's IEP goals.

- Use action songs, games, mirrors, and tactile activities to work on body or space problems.

- Work on balance and coordination of the upper and lower body for motor proficiency.

- Work with the student on obstacle courses to develop spatial orientation and perception.

- Use brightly colored objects for contrast between object and background.

- Provide opportunities for participation in rhythmic activities.

- Give brief instructions and have the student repeat them back to you.

Organizations

Division for Learning Disabilities (DLD), Council for Exceptional Children (CEC)
1110 North Glebe Rd., Ste. 300
Arlington, VA 22201-5704
703-620-3660
cec@cec.sped.org
www.dldcec.org

International Dyslexia Association (IDA) (formerly the Orton Dyslexia Society)
Chester Bldg., Ste. 382
8600 LaSalle Rd.
Baltimore, MD 21286-2044
800-222-3123
410-296-0232
info@interdys.org
www.interdys.org

Learning Disabilities Association of America (LDA)
4156 Library Rd.
Pittsburgh, PA 15234-1349
412-341-1515
info@ldaamerica.org
www.ldaamerica.org

National Center for Learning Disabilities (NCLD)
381 Park Ave. South, Ste. 1401
New York, NY 10016
888-575-7373
212-545-7510
www.ld.org

Recording for the Blind and Dyslexic (RFBD)
20 Roszel Rd.
Princeton, NJ 08540
866-732-3585
609-452-0606
custserv@rfbd.org
www.rfbd.org

Intellectual Disabilities

Definition

Intellectual disability is a term used when a person has certain limitations in mental functioning and in skills such as communicating, taking care of personal needs, and social skills. These limitations will cause a child to learn and develop more slowly than a child without intellectual disabilities. Children with intellectual disabilities may take longer to learn to speak, walk, and take care of personal needs such as dressing or eating. They are also likely to have trouble learning in school. They will learn many things, but it takes them longer, and there may be some things they cannot learn.

IDEA (1997) defines intellectual disabilities as "significantly subaverage general intellectual functioning, existing concurrently with deficits in adaptive behavior and manifested during the developmental period, that adversely affects a child's educational performance."

Doctors have found many causes of intellectual disabilities. The most common are the following.

- *Genetic conditions.* Sometimes intellectual disabilities are caused by abnormal genes inherited from parents, errors when genes combine, or other reasons. Examples of genetic conditions are Down syndrome, fragile X syndrome, and phenylketonuria (PKU).

- *Problems during pregnancy.* Intellectual disabilities can result when the baby does not develop properly inside the womb. For example, there may be a problem with the way the baby's cells divide as it grows. A woman who drinks alcohol or gets an infection like rubella during pregnancy may also have a baby with intellectual disabilities.

- *Problems at birth.* Babies who have problems during labor and birth, such as not getting enough oxygen, may have intellectual disabilities.

- *Health problems.* Diseases like whooping cough, measles, or meningitis can cause intellectual disability. Intellectual disability can also be caused by extreme malnutrition (not eating right), not getting enough medical care, or exposure to poisons like lead or mercury.

Intellectual disability is not a disease. It is also not a type of mental illness, like depression. There is no cure for intellectual disability. However, most children with intellectual disabilities can learn to do many things. It just takes them more time and effort than other children.

Diagnosis

Intellectual disability is diagnosed by looking at two main things:

- The ability of a person to learn, think, solve problems, and make sense of the world (called *IQ* or *intellectual functioning*)

- Whether the person has the skills necessary to live independently (called *adaptive behavior* or *adaptive functioning*)

Intellectual functioning, or IQ, is usually measured by an IQ test. The average score is 100. People scoring below 70 to 75 are thought to have intellectual disability. To measure adaptive behavior, professionals look at what a child can do in comparison to other children of the same age.

Certain skills are important to adaptive behavior, including the following:

- Daily living skills, such as getting dressed, going to the bathroom, and feeding oneself
- Communication skills, such as understanding what is said and being able to answer
- Social skills with peers, family members, adults, and others

To diagnose intellectual disability, professionals look at the person's mental abilities and adaptive skills. Providing services to help individuals with intellectual disabilities has led to a new understanding of intellectual disabilities. After the initial diagnosis of intellectual disability is made, professionals look at a person's strengths and weaknesses. They also look at how much support or help the person needs to get along at home, in school, and in the community. This approach gives a realistic picture of each individual. It also recognizes that this picture can change. As people grow and learn, their ability to get along in the world grows as well.

Characteristics

There are many signs of intellectual disability. For example, children with intellectual disabilities may

- sit up, crawl, or walk later than other children;
- learn to talk later or have trouble speaking;
- find it hard to remember things;
- not understand how to pay for things;
- have trouble understanding social rules;
- have trouble seeing the consequences of their actions;
- have trouble solving problems; or
- have trouble thinking logically.

About 87% of people with intellectual disabilities will only be a little slower than average in learning new information and skills. When they are children, their limitations may not be obvious. They may not even be diagnosed as having intellectual disabilities until they get to school. As they become adults, many people with mild intellectual disability can live independently. Other people may not even consider them as having intellectual disability.

The remaining 13% of people with intellectual disabilities score below 50 on IQ tests. These people will have more difficulty in school, at home, and in the community. People with more severe intellectual disabilities will need more intensive support their entire life. Every child with intellectual disabilities is able to learn, develop, and grow. With help, all children with intellectual disabilities can live a satisfying life.

Educational Implications

A child with intellectual disability can do well in school but is likely to need individualized help. Fortunately, states are responsible for meeting the educational needs of children with disabilities.

For children up to age 3, services are provided through an early intervention system. School staff members work with the child's family to develop an IFSP. The IFSP describes the child's unique needs as well as the services the child will receive to address those needs. The IFSP also emphasizes the unique needs of the family so that parents and other family members will know how to help their young child with intellectual disability. Early intervention services may be provided on a sliding-fee basis, meaning that the costs to the family will depend upon their income. In some states, early intervention services may be free.

For eligible school-aged children, including preschoolers, special education and related services are made available through the school system. School staff members work with the child's parents to develop an IEP, which describes the child's unique needs and the services that have been designed to meet those needs. Special education and related services are provided at no cost to parents.

Many children with intellectual disabilities need help with adaptive skills, which are skills needed to live, work, and play in the community. Teachers and parents can help a child work on these skills at both school and home. Some of these skills include the following:

- Communicating with others
- Taking care of personal needs (e.g., dressing, bathing, going to the bathroom)
- Health and safety
- Home living (e.g., helping to set the table, cleaning house, cooking dinner)
- Social skills (e.g., manners, knowing the rules of conversation, getting along in a group, playing a game)

- Reading, writing, and basic math
- As they get older, skills that will help them in the workplace

Supports or changes in the classroom help most students with intellectual disabilities. The following resources include ways to help children with intellectual disabilities.

Tips for Paraeducators

The following are a few tips for paraeducators when working with students with intellectual disabilities.

- Learn as much as you can about intellectual disability. The organizations listed at the end of this section will help you identify specific techniques and strategies to support the student educationally.
- Recognize that you can make an enormous difference in this student's life. Find out and emphasize the student's strengths and interests. Create opportunities for success.
- If you are not part of the student's IEP team, ask for a copy of the IEP. Educational goals will be listed there, as well as the services and classroom accommodations the student is to receive. Talk to specialists in your school (e.g., special educators) as necessary. They can help you identify effective methods of teaching the student, adapting the curriculum, and addressing the student's IEP goals in your classroom.
- Be as concrete as possible. Rather than just giving verbal directions, demonstrate what you mean. Rather than just relating new information verbally, show a picture. And rather than just showing a picture, provide the student with hands-on materials and experiences and the opportunity to try things out.
- Break longer tasks into small steps and demonstrate the steps. Have the student do the steps one at a time. Provide assistance as necessary.
- Give the student immediate feedback.
- Teach the student life skills such as daily living skills, social skills, and occupational awareness and exploration as appropriate. Involve the student in group activities or clubs.

- Work with the student's parents and other school personnel to create and implement an educational plan tailored to meet the student's needs. Regularly share information about how the student is doing at school and at home.
- Communicate and collaborate with the physical education teacher to implement the student's IEP goals.
- Be as concrete as possible with the student when explaining new tasks or giving directions so the student understands exactly what you want him or her to do.
- Use visual demonstrations often with the concrete directions.
- Use simple one- or two-word cues to reinforce what you want the student to do.
- When possible, pair the student with a peer educator who can model appropriate skill performance.
- Repeat and reinforce instructions and information as often as possible.
- Break each skill into step-by-step progressions, teaching the most simple step first and progressing from there.
- Reinforce appropriate behavior and correct skill performance.

Organizations

American Association on Intellectual and Developmental Disabilities (AAID)
444 North Capitol St. NW, Ste. 846
Washington, DC 20001-1512
800-424-3688
202-387-1968
www.aamr.org

The Arc of the United States
1010 Wayne Ave., Ste. 650
Silver Spring, MD 20910
301-565-3842
www.thearc.org

Division on Developmental Disabilities (DDD), Council for Exceptional Children (CEC)
1110 North Glebe Rd., Ste. 300
Arlington, VA 22201-5704
888-232-7733
703-620-3660
www.dddcec.org

Severe and Multiple Disabilities

Definition

People with severe disabilities traditionally have been labeled as having severe to profound intellectual disabilities. These individuals require ongoing, extensive support in more than one major life activity in order to participate in integrated community settings and enjoy the quality of life available to people with fewer or no disabilities. They frequently have additional disabilities, including movement difficulties, sensory losses, and behavior problems.

Characteristics

People with severe or multiple disabilities may exhibit a wide range of characteristics, depending on the combination and severity of disabilities and the person's age. There are, however, some traits they may share, including the following:

- Limited speech or communication
- Difficulty in basic physical mobility
- Tendency to forget skills through disuse
- Trouble generalizing skills from one situation to another
- A need for support in major life activities (domestic, leisure, community, and vocational activities)

Medical Implications

A variety of medical problems may accompany severe disabilities. Examples include seizures, sensory loss, hydrocephalus, and scoliosis. These conditions should be considered when establishing school services. A multidisciplinary team consisting of the student's parents, educational specialists, and medical specialists in the areas in which the student demonstrates problems should work together to plan and coordinate necessary services.

Educational Implications

In the past, students with severe or multiple disabilities were routinely excluded from public schools. Since the implementation of IDEA, public schools now serve large numbers of students with severe or multiple disabilities. Educational programming is likely to begin as early as infancy. At that time, as well as later on, the primary focus is increasing the child's independence.

In order to be effective, educational programs need to incorporate a variety of components to meet the considerable needs of individuals with severe or multiple disabilities. Programs should assess needs in four major areas: domestic, leisure and recreational, community, and vocational needs. These assessments enable the identification of functional objectives, which will result in the learner's increased skill and independence in dealing with the routine activities of daily life. Instruction should include training in expression of choice, communication, functional skill development, and age-appropriate social skills.

Related services are of great importance, and the multidisciplinary approach is crucial. Appropriate professionals such as speech and language therapists, physical and occupational therapists, and medical specialists need to work closely with classroom teachers and parents. Because of problems with skill generalization, related services are best offered during the natural routine in the school and community rather than removing the student from class for isolated therapy.

Frequently, classroom arrangements must take into consideration students' needs for medications, special diets, or special equipment. Adaptive aids and equipment enable students to increase their range of functioning. For example, in recent years computers have become effective communication devices. Other aids include wheelchairs, typewriters, head sticks (head gear), clamps, modified handles on cups and silverware, and communication boards. Computerized communication equipment and specially built vocational equipment also play important roles in adapting working environments for people with serious movement limitations.

Integration with peers without disabilities is another important component of the educational setting. Attending the same school and participating in the same activities as their peers without disabilities are crucial to the development of social skills and friendships for people with severe disabilities. Integration also benefits peers and professionals through positive attitude change.

Beginning as early as the elementary school years, community-based instruction is an important characteristic of educational programming. In order to increase the student's ability to generalize skills to appropriate situations, this type of instruction takes place in the actual setting where the skills will be used. As students grow older, more time is spent in the community; high school students may spend as much as 90% of their day there. Programs should draw on existing adult services in the community, including group homes, vocational programs, and recreational settings.

In light of the current Vocational Rehabilitation Act and the practice of supported employment, schools are now using school-to-work transition planning and working toward job placement in integrated, competitive settings rather than sheltered employment and day activity centers.

Tips for Paraeducators

The following are a few tips for paraeducators when working with students with severe or multiple disabilities.

- Communicate and collaborate with the physical education teacher to implement the student's IEP goals.
- Emphasize range-of-motion exercises.
- Have the student move as much as possible, either through independent movement or through hand-over-hand activities.
- Concentrate on postural righting activities.
- Use resistance training with exercise bands to develop muscle strength.
- Concentrate on vestibular activities.

Organizations

The Arc of the United States
1010 Wayne Ave., Ste. 650
Silver Spring, MD 20910
301-565-3842
info@thearc.org
www.thearc.org
www.thearcpub.com (for publications)

National Rehabilitation Information Center
    (NARIC)
4200 Forbes Blvd., Ste. 202
Lanham, MD 20706
800-346-2742
301-459-5900
naricinfo@heitechservices.com
www.naric.com

TASH (formerly The Association for Persons
    with Severe Handicaps)
1025 Vermont Ave. Floor 7
Washington, DC 20005
202-263-5600
info@tash.org
www.tash.org

United Cerebral Palsy (UCP)
1660 L St. NW, Ste. 700
Washington, DC 20005
800-872-5827
202-776-0406
202-973-7197 (TTY)
www.ucp.org

Visual Impairments

Definition

The terms *partially sighted, low vision, legally blind,* and *totally blind* are used in the educational context to describe students with visual impairments. They are defined as follows.

- *Partially sighted* indicates some type of visual problem that has resulted in a need for special education.
- *Low vision* generally refers to a severe visual impairment, not necessarily limited to distance vision. Low vision applies to all people with sight who are unable to read the newspaper at a normal viewing distance, even with the aid of eyeglasses or contact lenses. They use a combination of vision and other senses to learn, although they may require adaptations in lighting or the size of print and sometimes may use braille.
- *Legally blind* indicates that a person has less than 20/200 vision in the better eye or a very limited field of vision (20° at its widest point).
- Totally blind students learn via braille or other nonvisual media.

Visual impairment is the consequence of a functional loss of vision rather than the eye disorder itself. Eye disorders that can lead to visual impairments include retinal degeneration, albinism, cataracts, glaucoma, muscular problems that result in visual disturbances, corneal disorders, diabetic retinopathy, congenital disorders, and infection.

Characteristics

The effect of visual problems on a child's development depends on the severity, type of loss, age at which the condition appears, and overall functioning level of the child. Many children who have multiple disabilities may also have visual impairments resulting in delayed motor, cognitive, or social development.

A young child with visual impairments has little reason to explore interesting objects in the environment and thus may miss opportunities to have learning experiences. This lack of exploration may continue until learning becomes motivating or until intervention begins.

Because children with visual impairments cannot see parents or peers, they may be unable to imitate social behavior or understand nonverbal cues. Visual handicaps can create obstacles to a growing child's independence.

Educational Implications

Children with visual impairments should be assessed early so that they can benefit from early intervention programs, when applicable. Technology in the form of computers and optical and video aids enable many partially sighted, low vision, and blind children to participate in regular class activities. Large-print materials, books on tape, and braille books are also available.

Students with visual impairments may need additional help with special equipment and modifications in the regular curriculum to emphasize listening skills, communication, orientation and mobility, vocation and career options, and daily living skills. Students with low vision or those who are legally blind may need help in using their residual vision more efficiently and in working with special aids and materials. Students who have visual impairments combined with other types of disabilities have a greater need for an interdisciplinary approach and may require greater emphasis on self-care and daily living skills.

Tips for Paraeducators

The following are a few tips for paraeducators when working with students with visual impairments.

All fact sheets reprinted, by permission, from NICHCY. Available: www.nichcy.org.

- Communicate and collaborate with the physical education teacher to implement the student's IEP goals.
- Use other sensory modalities to provide information.
- Use a beeper or constant sound source to help the student orient to the goal or target.
- Place the student where it is easiest to hear instructions.
- Use contrasts between object and background if the student has some vision.
- Delineate play boundaries through gradation changes, cones, or other markers.
- Use a peer educator or partner to help the student perform a skill or participate in a game.
- Manually guide the student through the motor skill performance.
- Use audible balls when playing ball games.
- Use rope guide rails for bowling, running, and other activities.

Organizations

American Council of the Blind (ACB)
1155 15th St. NW, Ste. 1004
Washington, DC 20005
800-424-8666
202-467-5081
info@acb.org
www.acb.org

American Foundation for the Blind (AFB)
11 Penn Plaza, Ste. 300
New York, NY 10001
800-232-5463
800-232-3044 (for publications)
afbinfo@afb.net
www.afb.org

Blind Childrens Center (BCC)
4120 Marathon St.
Los Angeles, CA 90029
800-222-3566
323-664-2153
info@blindchildrenscenter.org
www.blindchildrenscenter.org

Appendix C

Special Education Acronyms

As in most professions, the special education community uses many acronyms when discussing services, assessments, and other topics regarding students with disabilities. The following is a list of common acronyms and what they mean.

APE—adapted physical education

CEC—Council for Exceptional Children

CP—cerebral palsy

CPR—consistency, persistency, relentlessness

DD—developmental disability

FBA—functional behavioral assessment

IDEA—Individuals with Disabilities Education Act

IEP—individual education program

ITP—individual transition plan

LD—learning disability

LRE—least restrictive environment

MR—mental retardation/intellectual disability

OT—occupational therapy

PBS—positive behavioral support

PT—physical therapy

SST—student study team

STO—short-term objective

VI—visual impairment

Appendix D

Physical Education Terminology

The following is a list of common terminology used in physical education.

age-appropriate activities—Activities appropriate for a chronological age, such as teaching fundamental skills to elementary children and specialized sport skills to adolescents.

assessment—Measuring and evaluating a student's performance.

corrective feedback—Information given to a student to correct motor skill performance.

criterion—Stated level of performance that indicates mastery of a skill.

developmentally appropriate—Activities that are appropriate to a student's level of cognitive, social, emotional, and physical development.

functional assessment—Assessment used to determine the student's functional abilities (skills needed for everyday life), such as dressing, eating, and the like.

individual differences—Students develop motor abilities at their own rate, which is influenced by heredity and environment.

leisure activities—Activities students partici-

pate in during their leisure time or time available when not working.

locomotor skills—Movement of the body from one location to another, such as hopping, running, jumping, and skipping.

nonlocomotor skills—Movement of the trunk or limbs while the feet remain stationary, such as bending, twisting, and stretching.

object-control (manipulative) skills—The ability to manipulate and control various objects, such as throwing, catching, and kicking balls.

perceptual motor development—The process of organizing new sensory information with stored information that leads to a movement response. Skills include such things as balance, cross-lateral integration, laterality, directionality, body image, and spatial awareness.

rubric—A set of criteria that measure a student's mastery of a motor skill or activity.

spatial awareness—Knowledge of how much space the body occupies and the body's relationship to other objects in space.

transition—Changing from one setting to another.

Appendix E

First Aid Information

Tonic-Clonic Seizures (Formerly Grand Mal)

Do the following:

- Protect the person from injury by removing nearby harmful objects.
- Cushion the person's head.
- Aid breathing by gently placing the person on one side in the recovery position once the seizure has finished.
- Be calm and reassuring.
- Stay with the person until recovery is complete.

Do not do the following:

- Restrain the person.
- Put anything in the person's mouth.
- Try to move the person unless danger is present.
- Give anything to eat or drink until the person is fully recovered.
- Attempt to bring them round or snap them out of the seizure. Allow the seizure to take its course.

Call for an ambulance if any of the following apply:

- You know it is the person's first seizure.
- The seizure continues for more than 5 minutes.
- One tonic-clonic seizure follows another without the person regaining consciousness between seizures.
- The person is injured during the seizure.
- You believe the person needs urgent medical attention.

External Bleeding Emergencies

- Help the student lie down.
- Apply direct pressure to the site of bleeding:
  - Place a clean dressing over the wound and apply direct pressure with your fingers or hand.
  - Once pressure is applied, keep it in place. If the dressing becomes soaked with blood, apply new dressings over the old. Continue as needed.
  - Do not disturb pads or bandages once bleeding is controlled.
- Raise the wound above the level of the heart if you do not suspect a fracture, continuing to apply direct pressure.
- If bleeding continues, apply pressure at a pressure point in the following places:
  - On the inside of the wrist (radial artery—where the pulse is checked)
  - On the inside of the upper arm (brachial artery)
  - On the crease in the groin (femoral artery)
- Apply a pressure bandage over the wound. (Note: When controlling major bleeding, it is not important to have sterile dressings, so use whatever you have at hand.)
- Give nothing by mouth.
- Seek medical aid if necessary (major bleeding emergency).

Breathing Emergency

- Check for responsiveness.
- If the person is not responsive, call for help.
- Determine if the person is breathing by using the look, listen, and feel method.
- Follow the ABCs:
    - Airway—Tip the head back and check for breathing at the same time.
    - Breathing—Give two full breaths. Keep the head tipped, pinch the nose, open your mouth wide, cover the person's mouth with your mouth, and blow hard into the lungs. Repeat.
    - Circulation—Check the pulse at the neck artery.
- If the person has a pulse but is not breathing, give rescue breathing. If there is no pulse, start CPR.
- Give one breath every 5 seconds.
- Recheck the pulse every minute; continue with breaths until help arrives.

Choking Emergency (Conscious Person)

- Determine if the person is choking.
- Call for help.
- Do abdominal thrusts:
    - Stand or kneel behind the person.
    - Wrap your arms around the waist.
    - Make a fist with one hand and put the thumb side of the fist against the middle of the abdomen, above the navel and below the tip of the breastbone.
    - Grasp your fist with your other hand.
    - Press your fist into the abdomen with a quick, upward thrust.
    - Repeat thrusts until the airway is clear.

Adapted Aquatics Information for Paraeducators

There are times when the paraeducator will accompany students to an aquatics setting during the school day or after-school programs. The information presented in this appendix will help paraeducators become aware of the issues that must be addressed in the pool area and locker room in regard to an adapted aquatics program. It is quite impossible for an aquatics instructor to teach, hold, encourage, and correct all of the students in a class at one time. It is imperative that paraeducators understand their crucial role in helping students with disabilities in the class. Without you, the aquatics instructor could not do it!

First, the instructor will need to know what your swimming ability is before the day that swimming begins. Send an e-mail or a note or call the instructor.

Beginning at the locker room, it is important to have the child use the toilet before putting the bathing suit on. A warm, soapy shower before coming onto the pool deck is necessary for everyone. This helps to prevent bacteria from entering the pool water and making people sick. Warm water and soap are especially important in the rear-end area. Disposable antibacterial wipes make an easy-to-use washcloth in this area. Remember to use gloves.

If a student has hair that will hang in the eyes while swimming, facilitate the use of a bathing cap or hair band.

Do not suit up a student who has open sores, a fever, a tracheotomy, an opened feeding tube, or a colostomy or who has had diarrhea in the past 24 hours. Students who have had diarrhea in the past week should have a warm, total-body soap shower before their bathing suits go on.

Students must never walk onto the pool deck alone. They should be supervised by a teacher or paraeducator in a ratio of at least two students to one adult. Physical support should be given or a water or pool wheelchair used for students whose mobility and balance are compromised.

The aquatics instructor should provide you with a specific plan for where you will go as soon as you enter the pool. Make sure you know where this is and communicate the directions to the student before you leave the locker area.

Be sure to place hearing aids, augmentative communication devices, glasses, and other assistive devices in a dry area away from the possibility of splashing.

Wait for the teacher's instructions before entering the pool.

Listen to the directions that the instructor gives to the students so that you understand and are able to enforce rules in the pool area. These rules are generally stricter than rules on land.

Ask your instructor for your responsibilities. Also, ask if there are any task cards or lesson plans that are laminated to take in the pool and if there are safety concerns that are specific to that day's plan.

While in the pool, don't act cold or complain that the water is not what you would like it to be. This rubs off on the students and creates behavior problems and noncompliance.

Generally, if the water is not warm enough for you, discuss this by e-mail or after school with the instructor, who may recommend that you wear a surf or rash-guard shirt or a wetsuit top. If you are not comfortable in a swimsuit, ask what the instructor would recommend. Most often it is OK to wear nylon, polyester, or lycra tops and shorts, but not cotton.

During your time in the water, help out in the way that the instructor has requested. Do not take time to do your own thing such as going off the diving board, snagging the best floatation tube for yourself to float around in, or swimming laps. It is not your time!

Be aware that if you are scheduled to hold a frightened swimmer, it is imperative not to let the swimmer drop under water or you will lose the swimmer's trust. A firm grip is required with frightened swimmers or novice swimmers with cerebral palsy.

Wear water shoes if they will help you to maintain a balanced and stable position as you assist the swimmers.

Created by Dr. Monica Lepore, master teacher of adapted aquatics.

Do not rush the swimmer to go under water if the swimmer is frightened. Consistent requests, demonstrations, and doing the skill with the student will bring results.

Please be patient in the swim area. Don't allow your excitement to translate into rushing students into something they might not be ready for. Follow the instructor's lesson and do not attempt to do a skill with the swimmer that the instructor has not introduced yet.

When leaving the pool, check to make sure you have all your students. Take attendance before, during, and after the swim session. Check the pool for stragglers before you go into the locker room.

Aquatics instructors cannot do this without you, and they truly appreciate your help.

Appendix G

Lifting and Transferring Students

General Tips

- Safety is the first concern.
  - This includes both the safety of the student and the person lifting the student.
    - Tell the person you are lifting what you plan to do before you do it.
- Make certain the wheelchair brakes are locked.
- Swing footrests out of the way as needed.
- Clear away any obstacles in your path.
- The distance the person is lifted should be as small as possible.
  - Bend your knees and lift with your legs.
  - Avoid bending and twisting at the same time; instead, stand and then pivot.
  - Use both hands to help lift.
  - If more than one person is lifting, make sure that you work together, with the leader giving commands.
- Wear suitable clothing and footwear when lifting—flat shoes are best.

Student Transferring Independently

- Be close by to assist if necessary.
- Encourage the student to transfer independently.

- Make sure wheelchair brakes are locked.
- Remove footrests.
- Clear the path.
- Give the student verbal cues for transfer (e.g., push up on arm rest, stand up, pivot, reach for support base).
- Help if needed.

One Person Transferring Student With Pivot Support

- Be sure wheelchair brakes are locked.
- Use a gait belt around the student's waist to give a firm surface to hold onto.
- The transfer surface should be at the same level or height that the student is transferring from.
- Move the footrests out of the way.
- Place the wheelchair at a 90° angle to the new surface, with the surfaces as close together as possible.
- Help the student scoot to the edge of the wheelchair.
- Place the student's feet flat on the floor.
- Place the student's arms around your upper back or elbows—not your neck.
- Place your hands on the gait belt.
- Count "One, two, three," while rocking forward on each number. Come to a standing position on "three" as you straighten your legs and lift the student from the wheelchair.

- When the student is upright and under control, pivot your feet toward the transfer surface, rotating the student as you pivot.
- Slowly lower the student's body onto the transfer surface. Have the student reach back to the new surface to help lower himself down.
- Hold onto the student until he is in a position that he can maintain himself.

Two People Transferring Student With Arms and Legs Lift

- Lock the wheelchair brakes.
- Move the footrests out of the way.
- First lifter: Stand behind the student. Help the student cross her arms over her chest. Place your arms under the student's upper arms.
- Second lifter: Place both hands under the student's lower thighs. Initiate and lead the lift at a prearranged count ("One, two, three, lift").
- Both lifters: Using your leg and arm muscles while bending your back as little as possible, gently lift the student's torso and legs at the same time.
- Move the student to the new surface. Position the student on the new surface, maintaining contact until the student is secure and safe.

Two People Transferring Student With Two-Side Lift

- Lock the wheelchair brakes.
- Move the footrests out of the way.
- Each lifter: Stand beside the student. Help the student cross his arms over his chest. Place your arm nearer the student's head around his back and your other arm under his thigh.
- Initiate and lead the lift at a prearranged count.
- Both lifters: Using your leg and arm muscles while bending your back as little as possible, gently lift the student's torso and legs at the same time.
- Move the student to the new surface. Position the student on the new surface, maintaining contact until the student is secure and safe.

University Programs Offering Adapted Physical Education Certification

At some time in the future you may decide to pursue a teaching degree. In particular, you may want to become an adapted physical education teacher. This appendix contains information on university programs that offer a major or minor in adapted physical education.

The following chart of higher education programs in APE can be found on the National Consortium of Physical Education and Recreation for Individuals with Disabilities Web site.

▶ **Adapted Physical Education (APE), Special Physical Education (SPE), and Adapted Physical Activity (APA) Higher Education Programs in the United States, 2006**

State	UG	G-M	G-D	APE-E/C	Online courses	School or university
AR		Yes			No	University of Arkansas Web site: www.uark.edu/depts/gradhkrd/M_PE_Adapted.html
CA	Yes	Yes	No		Yes	California State Polytechnic University, Pomona Web site: www.class.csupomona.edu/khp/programs.html#graduate
CA	Yes	Yes	No	Yes	No	California State University, Chico Web site: www.csuchico.edu/kine/ape/index.html
CA	Yes	Yes	No	Yes	No	California State University, Long Beach Web site: www.csulb.edu/programs/apa/
CA	Yes	No	No	Yes	No	California State University, Sacramento Web site: www.hhs.csus.edu/modells/
CA	Yes	Yes	No		No	California State University, San Bernardino Web site: http://kine.csusb.edu/
CA				Yes	No	California State University, Los Angeles Web site: www.calstatela.edu/dept/pe/
CA		Yes		Yes	No	Sonoma State University Web site: www.sonoma.edu/kinesiology/APE.html

(continued)

(continued)

State	UG	G-M	G-D	APE-E/C	Online courses	School or university
FL	No	Yes	No		Yes	University of Florida Web site: www.hhp.ufl.edu/faculty/cstopka/index.htm
HI	No	Yes	No		No	University of Hawaii at Manoa Web site: www.hawaii.edu/kls/pe/msape.html
IL	No	Yes	No		No	Northern Illinois University Web site: www3.niu.edu/knpe/programs/adapted.htm
IL		Yes			No	Southern Illinois University Edwardsville Web site: www.siue.edu/EDUCATION/kinesiology/specpe.html
IL		Yes			No	Western Illinois University Web site: www.wiu.edu/kinesiology/MSPE.html
IN		Yes	Yes		No	Indiana University Bloomington Web site: www.indiana.edu/~kines/graduate/index.shtml
IN	Yes	Yes	No		No	Ball State University Web site: www.bsu.edu/physicaleducation/
IN	Yes	No	No		No	Manchester College Web site: www.manchester.edu/Academics/Departments/ESS/index.htm
LA	Yes	Yes	No	Yes	No	Southeastern Louisiana University Web site: www.selu.edu/acad_research/depts/kin_hs/index.html
LA		Yes		Yes	No	University of New Orleans Web site: http://ed.uno.edu/~hphp/adaptedcurriculum.htm
MA	Yes	Yes			No	Bridgewater State University Web site: http://webhost.bridgew.edu/jhuber/mdtc.htm
MA		Yes			No	Springfield College Web site: www.spfldcol.edu/homepage/dept.nsf/academics/hper
MI	Yes	Yes	No		No	Eastern Michigan University Web site: www.emich.edu/hphp/
MI	Yes	Yes	No		No	Michigan State University Web site: http://edweb6.educ.msu.edu/kin/
MI	Yes	Yes	No	Yes	Yes	Saginaw Valley State University Web site: www.svsu.edu/phe/index.cfm
MI	No	No	Yes		No	University of Michigan Web site: www.kines.umich.edu/

State	UG	G-M	G-D	APE-E/C	Online courses	School or university
MI	Yes	Yes	No	Yes	No	Wayne State University Web site: www.kinesiology.wayne.edu/Physcial%20EducationGrad.html
MI	No	Yes	No		No	Western Michigan University Web site: www.wmich.edu/coe/hper/graduate/adaptedphysicaleducation.htm
MN	Yes	No	No	Yes	No	Bemidji State University Web site: www.bemidjistate.edu/Catalog/0204upcatalog/PE/adaptedlicense.html
MN	Yes	Yes	No	Yes	Yes	Minnesota State University, Mankato Web site: http://ahn.mnsu.edu/hp/
MN	Yes	No	No		No	Minnesota State University Moorhead Web site: www.mnstate.edu/admissions/fact_sheets/hpe.cfm
MN	Yes	Yes	No		No	St. Cloud State University Web site: www.stcloudstate.edu/hperss/default.asp
MN	No	Yes	No	Yes	No	University of Minnesota Web site: www.education.umn.edu/Kin/Kinesiology/MEd/dape.html
NC	No	Yes	No		No	East Carolina University Web site: www.ecu.edu/cs-hhp/exss/adapted-PE-curriculum.cfm
NC	No	Yes	No		No	North Carolina Agricultural and Technical State University Web site: www.ncat.edu/~schofed/SOE%20hper.htm
NC	No	Yes	No		No	North Carolina Central University Web site: www.nccu.edu/artsci/pe/grad.html
NE	Yes	Yes	No	Yes	Yes	University of Nebraska at Kearney Web site: http://aaunk.unk.edu/catalogs/current/dpt/dptpe.asp
NM	No	Yes	No		Yes	New Mexico State University Web site: http://education.nmsu.edu/nmsuape/
NM	No	Yes	No		No	University of New Mexico Web site: www.unm.edu/~adapted/
NV		Yes	Yes	Yes	No	University of Nevada Las Vegas Web site: http://education.unlv.edu/Sport_Ed/new_design/PA/index.html

(continued)

(continued)

State	UG	G-M	G-D	APE-E/C	Online courses	School or university
NY		Yes		Yes	No	Adelphi University Web site: http://education.adelphi.edu/hpe/physed/GRAD/
NY	Yes	No	No		No	Manhattan College Web site: http://manhattan.edu/academics/education/phys_ed/index.shtml
NY	Yes	Yes	No	Yes	No	State University of New York, Brockport Web site: www.brockport.edu/pes/
NY	Yes	Yes	No	Yes	Yes	State University of New York-Cortland Web site: www.cortland.edu/physed/
OH	No	Yes	Yes	Yes	No	The Ohio State University Web site: http://education.osu.edu/paes/tapes/default.htm
OH	Yes	No	No		No	Wright State University Web site: www.cehs.wright.edu:16080/academic/health_physed
OR	No	Yes	Yes		No	Oregon State University Web site: www.hhs.oregonstate.edu/nes/graduate/msd/index.html
PA	Yes	No	No		No	Slippery Rock University of Pennsylvania Web site: www.sru.edu/pages/9774.asp
PA				Yes	No	University of Pittsburg Web site: www.umc.pitt.edu/bulletins/graduate/edhealth.htm
PA	Yes	No	No		No	West Chester University of Pennsylvania Web site: http://health-sciences.wcupa.edu/kinesiology/Introduction.htm
RI	Yes	No	No		No	Rhode Island College Web site: www.ric.edu/hpe/
TX		Yes			No	Texas A&M University Web site: http://stpe.tamu.edu/
TX	Yes	Yes	Yes		Yes	Texas Woman's University Web site: www.twu.edu/hs/kines/ape.htm
UT	Yes	Yes	Yes		No	University of Utah Web site: http://www.health.utah.edu/ess/
VA	No	Yes	Yes		No	University of Virginia Web site: http://curry.edschool.virginia.edu/index.php
WI	Yes	No	No	Yes	No	University of Wisconsin-Eau Claire Web site: www.uwec.edu/KIN/minors/APE-desc.htm

State	UG	G-M	G-D	APE-E/C	Online courses	School or university
WI	Yes	Yes	No		No	University of Wisconsin-La Crosse Web site: www.uwlax.edu/sah/ess/sape/ugrad.htm
WI	Yes	No	No		Yes	University of Wisconsin-Madison Web site: www.education.wisc.edu/kinesiology/
WI	Yes	No	No		No	University of Wisconsin-Oshkosh Web site: www.uwosh.edu/adaptedpe/
WI	Yes	No	No		Yes	University of Wisconsin-Superior Web site: www.uwsuper.edu/%7Ehphp/
WI	Yes	No	No		No	University of Wisconsin-River Falls Web site: www.uwrf.edu/hhp/minors.html

UG = Undergraduate program; G-M = Master's program; G-D = Doctoral program; APE-E/C = Endorsement or certification

Selected Program Descriptions

University of Arkansas

This university offers a master of education degree in physical education with a concentration in APE. Students will complete 33 credit hours culminating their experience in either a master's degree project or a master's thesis.

Contact information:

Graduate Coordinator
Department of Health Science, Kinesiology, Recreation, and Dance
University of Arkansas
Fayetteville, AR 72701
Phone: 501-575-2858
Web site: www.uark.edu/depts/gradhkrd/M_PE_Adapted.html

California State University, Chico

CSU Chico offers a master of arts program in physical education (30 credit hours) with the option to complete a master's thesis or project, or a comprehensive examination. Students may take one of two courses of study for this program: APE and Pedagogy for individuals interested in teaching students with disabilities in school settings, and APE and Exercise Physiology for individuals who would like to work with adults with disabilities in community settings, and in either case, individuals may tailor their program of study to fit their needs and interests. This program also offers many service learning projects in the public schools and different Clinics and community programs such as the Autism clinic, KIDS:PLAY, and BE:WEL community programs.

Contact information:

Rebecca Lytle, PhD
Adapted Physical Activity Program Coordinator
California State University, Chico
Yolo Hall 262
400 West First Street
Chico, CA 95929
Phone: 530-898-4298
E-mail: rlytle@csuchico.edu
Web site: www.csuchico.edu/kine/ape/index.html

Sonoma State University

At Sonoma State, undergraduate physical education majors may seek to obtain a specialist credential in APE. Sonoma State also has a master of arts degree in APE that is tailored to fit the needs and interests of the student. Students graduating from this program will be able to demonstrate knowledge of their field of study, apply critical thinking and communication skills to various settings, understand research, develop responsibility and involvement at a professional level in their field, and be prepared to engage in profession-related dialogue at the culmination of the program.

Contact information:

Dr. Elaine McHugh
Sonoma State University
PE 16
1801 East Cotati Ave.
Rohnert Park, CA 94928
Phone: 707-664-2660
E-mail: elaine.mchugh@sonoma.edu
Web site: www.sonoma.edu/kinesiology/grad-program.html

California State University, Los Angeles

California State University Los Angeles offers an APE specialist credential that can be obtained concurrently with a degree in physical education but is also available for individuals who already hold a teaching credential in physical education or an equivalent credential. This program is completed in 36 credit hours and upon completion enables individuals to teach APE in the state of California.

Contact information:

Dr. Dwan Bridges
School of Kinesiology and Nutritional Science
5151 State University Drive
Los Angeles, CA 90032
Phone: 323-343-4658
E-mail: dbridge@calstatela.edu
Website: www.calstatela.edu/dept/pe/dept_pro.htm

California State University, Sacramento

California State University Sacramento offers an APE credential that can be taken in addition to or with courses in physical education. This program can be completed in 21 credit hours but may take more for an individual who is not a physical education major, as there are prerequisite courses that are necessary to obtain the credential.

Contact information:

Fred Baldini, Department Chair
Sacramento State
6000 J Street
Sacramento, CA 95819-6073
Phone: 916-278-6441
E-mail: baldinif@csus.edu

Web site: http://aaweb.csus.edu/catalog/current/PROGRAM/Kins.asp

University of Florida

The University of Florida offers a master of science degree (36 credit hours) with a specialization in adapted physical activity. Students can elect to complete a master's thesis, project, or a non-thesis option. The University of Florida also offers two online courses for individuals seeking further education through distance education: adapted physical activity and medical and health aspects for individuals with disabilities. Both courses are offered in the fall, spring, and summer semesters and prepare individuals to take the APENS national examination.

Contact information:

Chris Stopka
Department of Health Education & Behavior
P.O. Box 118210
University of Florida
Gainesville, FL 32611-8210
Phone: 352-392-0583 ext. 1259
Fax: 352-392-1909
E-mail: cstopka@hhp.ufl.edu
Web site: www2.hhp.ufl.edu/heb
Online courses: www.hhp.ufl.edu/depts/distance/adaptedphysicalactivityemailnewsletter
www.hhp.ufl.edu/depts/distance/medicaland-healthaspectsemailnewsletter

University of Hawai'i at Manoa

The University of Hawai'i at Manoa offers its students a master of science degree in kinesiology and leisure science with a specialization in physical education/adapted physical education (PE/APE). This is a two- to three-year program that provides students with research opportunities, field experiences, and advanced knowledge/skills in PE/APE. Exit requirements include at least 30 credit hours, and completion of a comprehensive examination and the APENS national exam.

Contact information:

Nathan M. Murata, PhD
Department & Graduate Chairperson
Department of Kinesiology and Leisure Science
1337 Lower Campus Road
PE/A Complex, Room 231
Honolulu, HI 96822
Office: 808-956-3807
Fax: 808-956-7976

E-mail: nmurata@hawaii.edu
Web site: www.catalog.hawaii.edu/schoolscol-
    leges/education/grad.htm

Northern Illinois University

NIU offers a master of science degree in physical education with the option of completing a specialization in APE. The program is designed to prepare individuals to teach physical education to students with disabilities as well as to perform roles specific to APE consultation and culminates in a master's thesis, master's project, or master's interdisciplinary inquiry in 31 credit hours of study.

Contact information:

Paul Carpenter
Phone: 815-753-8284
E-mail: knpe@niu.edu
Web site: www3.niu.edu/knpe

Southern Illinois University Edwardsville

The program at SIUE provides students with a master of science in education degree with a major in kinesiology (33 credits total). Within that concentration, students may focus their program of study on special physical education, and it is open to graduate students with and without teaching backgrounds. Students graduating from the SIUE program have the option to complete a comprehensive written exam or the Adapted Physical Education National Standards (APENS) exam.

Contact information:

E. William Vogler, EdD
Professor and Chairperson
Department of Kinesiology and Health Education
Southern Illinois University Edwardsville
Campus Box 1126
Edwardsville, IL 62026
Phone: 618-650-2984
E-mail: wvogler@siue.edu
Web site: www.siue.edu/GRADUATE/catalog/
    CH2/EDU/kinesio.html

Western Illinois University

Western Illinois University offers a master of science degree in kinesiology with a focus on APE. Students will have completed one of three options upon graduation: a master's thesis (32 semester credit hours), a comprehensive exam (38 semester credit hours), or a synthesis paper of an internship experience (38 semester credit hours).

Contact information:

Christopher Kovacs
Kinesiology 220C Brophy Hall
Macomb, IL 61455-9960
Phone: 309-298-1981
Fax: 309-298-2981
Department e-mail: kinesiology @wiu.edu
Web site: www.wiu.edu/grad/catalog/kinesiol-
    ogy.php

Indiana University Bloomington

The IUB program offers a master of science or doctor of philosophy degree with a concentration in adapted physical education (36 credits total). If master's students possess a teaching degree, graduates will be able to apply for certification in APE. Courses in this curriculum offer students the latest information in the field of APE. Students in this program have the option to complete a master's thesis (additional credit hours are required for this option) or the options to take the APENS exam or a comprehensive exam.

Contact information:

Dr. Georgia Frey or Dr. Frances (Mike) Kozub
Associate Dean for Academic Program Admin-
    istration
School of Health, Physical Education, and
    Recreation
HPER 121
Indiana University
Bloomington, IN 47405-4801
Phone: 812-855-1561
E-mail: HPER@indiana.edu
Web site: www.indiana.edu/~kines/graduate/
    index.shtml

Ball State University

Ball State University provides its students with a master of art or a master of science degree with a specialization in adapted physical education. The mission of the adapted physical education specialization is to provide students a link between the theory learned in the course work and the practical side of APE. Students also have the opportunity to work in different practicum sites as well as to participate in research dealing with individuals with disabilities.

Contact information:

Graduate Coordinator
Sport and Physical Education Graduate Programs
School of Physical Education, Sport, and
    Exercise Science
Muncie, IN 47306
Phone: 765-285-1462
Fax: 765-285-3485
Web site: www.bsu.edu/physicaleducation/
    graduate/

Manchester College

Manchester College offers an undergraduate physical education degree with a certification in APE. Students have the option to complete this certification along with a teaching certification upon graduation.

Contact information:

Dr. Lana Groombridge
604 E. College Avenue
North Manchester, IN 46962
Phone: 260-982-5353
E-mail: LLGroombridge@manchester.edu
Web site: www.manchester.edu

University of New Orleans

This APE specialization program prepares individuals to teach children with disabilities in APE settings. This program provides a number of courses as well as experiences teaching students with disabilities to its graduate students (33-36 credits total). Students will graduate with a master of education degree with a certification to teach APE.

Contact information:

Lorelei Cropley, PhD, RN
Associate Professor, Graduate Coordinator
University of New Orleans
Lakefront
2000 Lakeshore Drive
New Orleans, LA 70148
Phone: 504-280-6421
E-mail: lcropley@uno.edu
Web site: http://ed.uno.edu/~hphp/adapted-
    curriculum.htm

Bridgewater State University

Bridgewater State University offers a bachelor of science degree and a master of science degree in physical education with a concentration in APE. The concentration in APE prepares individuals to work with students who have unique needs and to meet the needs of these students. Practicum experiences are offered both on and off campus in order to prepare individuals to work in a variety of settings post graduation. Students in the master's program will take 27 to 33 credit hours in addition to core physical education courses to obtain the concentration in APE.

Contact information:

Robert Haslam
Movement Arts, Health Promotion & Leisure
    Studies
Bridgewater State College
Tinsley Center, Rm. 232
Bridgewater, MA 02325
Phone: 508-531-1215
Fax: 508-531-1717
E-mail: rhaslam@bridgew.edu
Website: http://www.bridgew.edu/MAHPLS/

Springfield College

Springfield College offers a master of science degree with a concentration in adapted physical education.

Contact information:

Donald Shaw, Jr.
Department of Health, PE & Recreation
263 Alden Street
Springfield, MA 01109
Phone: 413-748-3225
Fax: 413-748-3024
E-mail: admissions@springfieldcollege.edu
Web site: www.spfldcol.edu/home.nsf/acade-
    mics/graduate

Eastern Michigan University

Eastern Michigan offers a master of science degree in physical education interdisciplinary adapted physical education (PEAD). Students will be able to complete their degree by taking APE courses both at Eastern Michigan and Michigan State University in 33 credit hours with the option to complete a master's thesis or master's project.

Contact information

Dr. Ian R. Haslam
Department Head
School of Health Promotion and Human Per-
    formance
Eastern Michigan University
Ypsilanti, MI 48197

Phone: 734-487-7120 ext. 4388
E-mail: ian.haslam@emich.edu
Website: www.emich.edu/coe/catalogs/grad/
hperd/mspe_ia.html

Western Michigan University

Western Michigan offers a master of arts degree with an emphasis on special/APE. In this program, students are prepared by completing 36 hours of required course work and a master's thesis in order to graduate and receive certification as an APE teacher in the state of Michigan. Students have the option to receive a minor in APE from Western Michigan to become a certified APE teacher.

Contact information:

Dr. Jiabei Zhang
4024 Student Recreation Center
Western Michigan University
Kalamazoo, MI 49008-5426
Phone: 269-387-2949
Fax: 269-387-2704
E-mail: ZHANGJ@wmich.edu
Web site: www.wmich.edu/coe/hper/graduate/
index.htm

Michigan State University

Students in this program receive a master of science degree with a concentration in adapted physical activity. With this degree, students may work in many different fields such as coaching and teaching individuals with disabilities, and prepares students for doctoral study as well. Students in the master's degree program complete part of their course work at Eastern Michigan University in a joint degree program. Students will complete 30 semester credit hours culminating in one of four experiences: (a) master's thesis, (b) master's project, (c) internship (60 hours per semester credit), or (d) comprehensive examination. Students are expected to show evidence of professional involvement, demonstrate their teaching effectiveness within an APA setting, and know and understand the role of research in an APA setting.

Contact information:

Department of Kinesiology
138 IM Sports Circle
Michigan State University
East Lansing, MI 48824-1049
Web site: http://edweb6.educ.msu.edu/kin/
academics/ms/MSadapted2.htm

Saginaw Valley State University

This program offers a master of arts in teaching (MAT) to already endorsed individuals in special education or PETE (36 credits). In addition, the program offers an endorsement in APE (19 credits) to prepare prospective and current teachers to become effective in teaching individuals with disabilities as direct service providers or as a collaborative team member in the schooling process for individuals with disabilities. Individuals completing this program will become certified adapted physical educators through taking the APENS national examination.

Contact information:

Dr. Robert Pratt and Dr. Jennifer Bridges
Coordinators, Physical Education Teacher
Education
7400 Bay Road
University Center, MI 48710
Phone: 989-964-4622; 989-964-7324
E-mail: rpratt@svsu.edu; bridges@svsu.edu
Web site: www.svsu.edu/phe/me.cfm

Wayne State University

At Wayne State University, students have the option of completing an APE endorsement. In this case, potential students must hold a valid Michigan teaching certificate in physical education or special education along with a baccalaureate degree. Students in the endorsement program will take 12 credits of courses in APE and 12 in approved special education courses.

Contact information:

Jeffrey Martin
Kinesiology, Health and Sport Studies
265 Matthaei Physical Education Center
Wayne State University
Detroit, MI 48202
Phone: 313-577-1381
E-mail: aa3975@wayne.edu
Web site: www.bulletins.wayne.edu/gbk-
output/edu8.html

Minnesota State University Mankato

The student's program of study is determined by the type of degree they seek (master of arts or master of science), but Minnesota State University Mankato allows their students to design the course of study to fit their needs in developmental/adapted physical education (D/APE).

Students have the option to complete a thesis or an alternate plan paper to be eligible to graduate. To obtain licensure in D/APE the student must first have an undergraduate teaching degree in physical education.

Contact information:

Dr. Sherry Folsom-Meek, Coordinator
Minnesota State University
228 Wiecking Ctr.
Mankato, MN 56001-6062
Phone: 507-389-2626
E-mail: sherry.folsom-meek@mnsu.edu
Web site: http://ahn.mnsu.edu/hp/graduate/dape.html

St. Cloud State University

St. Cloud offers a master of science degree in physical education with an emphasis on developmental/APE. Students may choose one of two plans to complete their degree: Plan A requires the students to write a master's thesis and can be completed in 30 semester credit hours, while plan B requires the students to finish a master's paper and take an oral examination over the paper. Plan B can be completed in 33 semester credit hours, and both plans may be for full- or part-time students.

Contact information:

Department of Health, Physical Education, Recreation, and Sport Science
327 Halenbeck Hall
St. Cloud, MN 56301
Phone: 320-308-2155
Fax: 320-308-5399
E-mail: hperss@stcloudstate.edu
Web site: http://bulletin.stcloudstate.edu/gb/programs/PhysicalEducation.asp

University of Minnesota

This program offers a license/additional license in developmental and APE (D/APE). This licensure can be completed in 19 credit hours that can also be applied to a master of education degree in applied kinesiology for a total of 30 credit hours.

Contact information:

School of Kinesiology
1900 University Ave. SE
Minneapolis, MN 55455
Phone: 612-625-5300
Fax: 612-626-7700

E-mail: kin@umn.edu
Web site: www.education.umn.edu/Kin/Kinesiology/MEd/dape.html

North Carolina Central University

Students attending NCCU will graduate with a master of science degree in APE. The program is designed to tie theory to practice in working with individuals with varying disabilities in many practicum settings. Students will complete 36 semester credit hours and must have an undergraduate degree in physical education or a similar/related field to be admitted into the program, and will complete the program by writing a master's thesis.

Contact information:

Chairperson
Department of Physical Education and Recreation
P.O. Box 19542
North Carolina Central University
Durham, NC 27707
Phone: 919-560-6186 or 919-530-5383
E-mail: politano@wpo.nccu.edu
Web site: www.nccu.edu/artsci/pe/grad.html

East Carolina University

East Carolina University offers a master of arts and master of education degree in APE. In 36 semester hours, students will be able to tie theory to practice by working in a variety of practicum experiences with individuals with different disabilities. This program prepares students to teach individuals with disabilities as well as to act as a consultant in the education process. Students have the option to work on a thesis or non-thesis track in this program.

Contact information:

Dr. James Decker
168 Minges Coliseum
Greenville, NC 27858
Phone: 252-328-0001
E-mail: deckerj@mail.ecu.edu
Web site: www.ecu.edu/cs-hhp/programs.cfm

New Mexico State University

New Mexico State offers students a master of arts in education degree with a graduate minor in APE. The mission of this program is to provide individualized instruction to individuals with disabilities and to provide the students at NMSU with the knowledge and abilities to appropriately teach and plan for teaching individuals with disabilities. The program is based on the APENS national standards, with the goal to graduate certified APE (CAPE) teachers. This program also offers one online course titled Adapted Physical Education National Standards Professional Preparation for those who may not live near the university.

Contact information:

Scott J. Pedersen, PhD, CAPE
Assistant Professor
Director, NMSUAPE Program
Physical Education, Recreation and Dance
    Department
New Mexico State University
P.O. Box 30001 MSC-3M
Las Cruces, NM 88003
E-mail: pedersen@nmsu.edu
Web site: http://education.nmsu.edu/nmsuape/

University of Nevada Las Vegas

UNLV offers both a master of science and master of education in sports education leadership degree with a concentration in APE/APE endorsement (36 semester credit hours). The master of science program is a thesis track program, while the master of education program is a non-thesis track program culminating in a project or written exam. This university also offers a doctor of philosophy degree in sports education with a concentration in APE, which requires 66 hours of courses beyond the master's degree.

Contact information:

University of Nevada Las Vegas
Department of Sports Education Leadership
4505 Maryland Parkway
P.O. Box 453031
Las Vegas, NV 89154-3031
Phone: 702-895-5057
Fax: 702-895-5056
Web site: http://education.unlv.edu/Sport_Ed/
    new_design/grad.html

State University of New York College at Cortland

SUNY Cortland offers its students a master of science in education in physical education with a specialization in APE. The mission of this program is to develop individuals who are well rounded and knowledgeable agents of change. The specialization focuses on the APENS national standards and prepares individuals to work with students with varying disabilities. Individuals in this program will complete 30 credit hours cumulating in either a thesis or comprehensive examination.

Contact information:

Jerry Casciani
Department Chair
Department of Physical Education
E 255 Park Center
SUNY Cortland
P.O. Box 2000
Cortland, NY 13045
Phone: 607-753-5577
E-mail: cascianij@cortland.edu
Web site: www.cortland.edu/physed/APEGrad-
    Program.htm

Adelphi University

Adelphi offers a master of arts degree in physical education with an emphasis on APE accompanied by an Adelphi certificate in APE. The program is designed to improve teaching skills, offer research opportunities, and introduce students to the many career opportunities in APE. The program of study can be designed to meet the needs and interests of the student.

Contact information:

Adelphi University
Department of Health Studies, Physical Edu-
    cation, and Human Performance Science
Woodruff Hall, Gymnasium
1 South Avenue
P.O. Box 701
Garden City, NY 11530-0701
Phone: 516-877-4260
Fax: 516-877-4258
Web site: http://education.adelphi.edu/hpe/
    physed/GRAD/

The State University of New York, College at Brockport

SUNY Brockport prides itself in being the first university to offer specialization in APE across the country in 1968. Students in this program complete a number of practicum and field experiences throughout their educational process at SUNY Brockport. Recently, SUNY Brockport has received a federal grant from the U.S. Department of Education to provide scholarships for graduate students seeking a degree in APE. Potential students seeking professional certification need to have a teaching certificate in physical education, while non-certification students should have completed at least 12 semester hours of physical education–related course work. Students will graduate with a master of science degree with a concentration in APE or early childhood APE (30 semester credits total).

Contact information:

Joseph P. Winnick, EdD
Department of Physical Education & Sport
SUNY College at Brockport
350 New Campus Drive
Brockport, NY 14420-2994
Phone: 585-395-2383
E-mail: JWinnick@brockport.edu
Web site: www.brockport.edu/pes/adapted/
    overview.doc

The Ohio State University, Main Campus

The mission of the APE program at OSU is to provide its students with opportunities to work with individuals with disabilities in various community settings as well as through various research projects. OSU offers its students master of arts (53-60 credits total) and doctor of philosophy degrees in adapted physical education. Prospective students who are current physical education teachers may also work toward an Ohio endorsement certificate in APE. Students completing the master's degree and endorsement certificate take the APENS national certification exam and master's students must also complete a comprehensive exam or thesis in order to graduate. Both the master's and doctoral students have the opportunity to work in various settings with individuals with disabilities as well as to teach and supervise undergraduate students in a lab setting.

Contact information:

David Porretta, PhD
The Ohio State University
1760 Neil Avenue
Pomerene Hall, Room 202
Columbus, OH 43210
Phone: 614-292-0849

Fax: 614-292-7229
E-mail: porretta.1@osu.edu
Web site: www.coe.ohio-state.edu/degreespro-
    grams/gradPrograms.cfm

Wright State University

Wright State offers an undergraduate major in APE. In this program students are given the necessary knowledge to become effective teachers and are given many opportunities to apply the knowledge in a variety of practicum experiences working with individuals with disabilities.

Contact information:

Dr. Willie Gayle
3640 Colonel Glenn Highway
316 Nutter Center
Dayton, OH 45435
Phone: 937-775-2615
E-mail: willie.gayle@wright.edu
Web site: www.cehs.wright.edu/academic/
    health_physed/adapted_physed/index.php

Oregon State University

Oregon State offers a master of science degree in movement studies in disability and a doctor of philosophy in exercise and sport science degree in movement studies in disability. Both programs are designed to help graduates to work effectively with individuals with disabilities in their motor and fitness needs as well as participate in various research projects. This program provides in-depth theory classes which the students have the opportunity to put into practice in different field experiences working with individuals with disabilities.

Contact information:

Jeff McCubbin
College of Health and Human Sciences
Oregon State University
123A Women's Building
Corvallis, OR 97331-5109
Phone: 541-737-5921
Fax: 541-737-4230
E-mail: jeff.mccubbin@oregonstate.edu
Web site: www.hhs.oregonstate.edu

University of Pittsburgh

The University of Pittsburgh offers a certificate in APE that targets health and physical education teachers to enhance their knowledge and skills for teaching students with disabilities as well as to facilitate inclusion within their general education classes. Individuals seeking to complete the APE certification process must take 24 credit hours that include at least six credits in the core specialization.

Contact information:

Graduate Coordinator
Department of Health and Physical Activity
140 Trees Hall
Pittsburgh, PA
Phone: 412-648-8320
Fax: 412-648-7092
E-mail: hpred@pitt.edu
Web site: www.umc.pitt.edu/bulletins/graduate/edhealth.htm

Texas A&M University

This program offers master of education and master of science degrees in adapted physical education; potential master's students are encouraged to have teaching experience prior to entering the program.

Contact information:

Ron McBride (Pedagogy) 979-845-8788
Stephen Dorman (Department Head) 979-845-1333
Department of Kinesiology
Texas A&M University
College Station, TX 77843
Phone: 979-845-3209
Web site: http://stpe.tamu.edu/grd1.htm

Texas Woman's University

TWU offers its students a master of science degree in APE as well as a doctor of philosophy degree in adapted physical activity (APA). The master's degree program is a 36 credit hour program cumulating in a master's thesis or non-thesis project, professional portfolio, and completing the APENS national exam; this program is possible to complete in one calendar year. The emphasis of this program is on preparing students to work with individuals with low incidence disabilities in the least restrictive environment. The PhD program offers students many opportunities to complete projects and make presentations to build their professional portfolio. Students completing this well-known doctoral program are identified as highly qualified teacher educators in APA. It is recommended that potential doctoral students

have a minimum of two years of teaching experience prior to entering the program.

Contact information:

Dr. Ronald French
Dept. of Kinesiology, Pioneer Hall 208
P.O. Box 425647
Denton, TX 76204-5647
Phone: 940-898-2582
Fax: 940-898-2581
E-mail: RFrench@twu.edu
Web site: www.twu.edu/hs/kines/g_program_phd_ape.htm

University of Utah

The University of Utah offers both a master of science and doctor of philosophy degree in special physical education. The two-year master's program is designed to develop teaching skills through a series of practicum experiences in order to develop an effective special physical education teacher and both a thesis (32 credit hours) and non-thesis (36 credit hours) program of study is available. The doctoral program emphasizes research and practicum experiences to provide future teacher educators who are knowledgeable in the field both in theory and practice.

Contact information:

Hester L. Henderson, PhD
Director of Special Physical Education Program
University of Utah
Department of Exercise and Sport Science
250 South 1850 East Room 241
Salt Lake City, UT 84112-0920
Phone: 801-581-7964
E-mail: hester.henderson@health.utah.edu
Web site: www.health.utah.edu/ess/graduate/physEd

University of Virginia

The University of Virginia offers several graduate programs in APE. The master of education in APE focuses heavily on practical experiences where master's students teach APE in the surrounding public schools; this program can be completed in just over one year—two summers and two semesters (fall and spring). In addition, the University of Virginia offers doctor of philosophy and doctor of education degrees in APE. The doctor of philosophy degree program focuses heavily on research in preparing doctoral students to teach at research one institutions of higher education. The doctor of education degree program focuses on research as well as preparing doctoral students to be professors in teacher-training universities.

Contact information:

Luke Kelly
University of Virginia
Memorial Gymnasium 221
Charlottesville, VA 22904-4261
Phone: 434-243-2314
E-mail: lek@virginia.edu
Web site: http://curry.edschool.virginia.edu/
    kinesiology/adaptpe/

University of Wisconsin at LaCrosse

The University of Wisconsin at LaCrosse offers a master of science degree in physical education teaching with a special populations emphasis (35 credits total). The mission of the Special Populations Programs at UWL is to provide many community-based physical activity and physical education programs by preparing students to be direct service providers to individuals with disabilities. Individuals who complete the program will be eligible to receive APE specialist certification. Master's students in this program receive courses in assessment, teaching methods, specific disabilities, curriculum development, and supervision as well as a variety of clinical experiences.

In the graduate certification in special physical education program (18 credits total), full-time physical education teachers are able to complete their APE certificate in only three summers. At the completion of this program, students will be eligible to receive the add-on certificate in APE. This program provides teachers who currently teach individuals with disabilities with necessary skills and abilities to effectively teach students with disabilities.

Contact information:

Dr. Manny Felix and Dr. Garth Tymeson
114 Wittich Hall
UW at La Crosse
La Crosse, WI 54601
Phone: 608-785-8691
Fax: 608-785-8206
E-mail: specialpops@uwlax.edu; felix.emma@
    uwlax.edu; tymeson.gart@uwlax.edu
Web site: www.uwlax.edu/sah/ess/sape/grad.htm

University of Wisconsin Oshkosh

The University of Wisconsin Oshkosh has developed a minor in APE to ultimately certify prospective teachers with an APE license for Wisconsin and also to prepare students with the necessary course work to take the APENS national examination. The minor can be completed in 26 credit hours.

Contact information:

Dr. Robert Weber
Department of Kinesiology & Health
Kolf Physical Education Center
UW Oshkosh
800 Algoma Blvd.
Oshkosh, WI 54901
Phone: 920-424-1231
E-mail: schmidtw@uwosh.edu; weberr@
    uwosh.edu
Web site: www.uwosh.edu/adaptedpe

Ideas for Increasing Physical Activity

As many people are aware, there is a growing obesity epidemic in our country among both children and adults. Children with disabilities are also affected by this epidemic. Prevention is the key to combating overweight and obesity. The following list describes some ways the paraeducator can embed activity into the everyday schedules of children with disabilities.

Pedometers

Have students wear pedometers to increase their walking distance. They can be used as motivation in and outside of school.

Playground

Motivate and help the students to become actively involved on the playground equipment. Have them fully engage in the movement choices of the playground equipment, such as climbing, balancing, swinging, walking (in, over, under, through), and sliding. In addition, encourage them to more fully interact with their peers during recreational playground games. This will also help to develop their interpersonal and socialization skills.

Classroom

Have students retrieve materials or equipment needed for the class lesson. They can also help set up the classroom environment for the day's instruction so they are more active, involved, independent, and responsible.

Walk

Help students walk the stairs instead of using the elevator. If a student uses a wheelchair but can walk, take the time to help the student walk to increase activity.

Independence

If students use a wheelchair, encourage them to propel themselves with their feet or ambulate in a way that uses energy. Some alternatives may be a scooterboard, tricycle, or handcycle.

After School

Encourage your student to become involved in after-school activities such as intramurals, sports, and recreation programs. They can also join the safety patrol, marching band, or any type of school-related activities to increase physical activity level.

Family

Discuss the student's need for additional physical activity with the student's parents or care providers. Encourage them to enroll the student in available community or church activities or purchase recreational equipment that will facilitate more physical activity. Some suggestions include handcycles, adapted bicycles or tricycles, basketball hoops, bocce games, and roller skates.

Appendix J

Confidentiality

Records and information about children with disabilities must be treated with confidentiality. In other words, the child's personal information is to be distributed only to professionals who must know the information to safely and successfully teach that child. The information obtained by any teacher, paraeducator, or therapist must also be kept confidential between teachers and specialists on the multidisciplinary team.

Policies

- The Americans with Disabilities Act (ADA) and section 504 of the Rehabilitation Act require that all disability information be kept confidential.

- The U.S. Department of Education regulations state that any documentation of a disability must be kept separate from other records.

- Records must be kept alone so that there are no other records with them that people might need to look through (in order to ensure confidentiality).

- These rules ensure that disability-related information is medical information and is not subject to the Family Educational Rights and Privacy Act (FERPA) of 1974.

- Information cannot be released to anyone without the required documentation.

- Copies of records cannot be released unless there is written consent from the individual and from the professional who wrote the original report.

- All conversations regarding a student's disability should be conducted privately unless the student brings it up.

Obtaining Records

- Records can be obtained with the student's consent or, if the student is under the age of 18, with the parents' consent.

- Students are free to tell whomever they want to tell about their disabilities.

- Legal obligation includes such circumstances as a court subpoena, a valid search warrant, or other legislated requirements as may be in force at any given time.

- Information can also be released if someone else's life is in danger.

- Some teachers may need to know certain details about the disability so that if something is happening to the student, they will know how to react. This information is given on a need-to-know basis.

- Any physical education teacher or paraeducator who directly teaches a child with a disability has the right to the child's records to ensure that they know the child's strengths and weaknesses. They also need to know about any safety precautions that need to be taken.

99 Ways to Say "Very Good"

When teaching children with or without disabilities, it is very important to know how to give positive feedback. There are so many ways to tell children that they had a good try or they did a nice job. The following list is a start to ensure that the instructor and paraeducator do not run out of ways to say "Good job."

You're on the right track now.	That's not half bad.	That's great.
You've got it made.	Nice going.	Superb.
I'm proud of the way you worked today.	You've just about mastered that.	You're really learning a lot.
You're really working hard today.	You've got your brain in gear today.	You outdid yourself today.
You've just about got it.	That's the way.	Good remembering.
You're doing a good job.	Wow.	Right on.
Super.	That's the way to do it.	You're improving.
That's the best you've ever done.	Now that's what I call a fine job.	I've never seen anyone do it better.
That's it.	Keep up the good work.	You're doing beautifully.
Congratulations.	You haven't missed a thing.	Keep it up.
That's right.	Sensational.	You've got that down pat.
That's good.	That's better.	Way to go.
That's coming along nicely.	Nothing can stop you now.	Good thinking.
Good work.	That was first-class work.	Keep on trying.
I'm happy to see you working like that.	You must have been practicing.	You're quick to learn.
Not bad.	Wonderful.	Good for you.
You are doing that much better today.	Congratulations. You got (number of behaviors) right.	That's really nice.
Now you have it.	Much better.	Good going.

(continued)

(continued)

Exactly right.	That's better than ever.	Look at you go.
I knew you could do it.	Excellent.	Marvelous.
Great.	Perfect.	That's it.
Now you've figured it out.	Fine.	I like that.
Keep working on it, you're getting better.	That's good—I like it.	You are awesome, and you did an awesome job.
That's much better.	Terrific.	That's good, [name of student].
Good for you.	You're really going to town.	I think you've got it now.
Couldn't have done it better myself.	Now you've got it.	It's a pleasure to teach when you work like that.
You make it look easy.	Nice going.	Good job, [name of student].
You really make my job fun.	Outstanding	You figured that out fast.
That's the right way to do it.	Fantastic.	You remembered.
One more time and you'll have it.	Good remembering.	That kind of work makes me very happy.
That's quite an improvement.	Tremendous.	Now you have the hang of it.
You're getting better every day.	That's a job well done.	You certainly did well today.
You did it that time.	You did that very well.	You're doing fine.

References and Resources

References

Aschemeier, A. (2004). *The role of paraprofessionals in physical education.* Unpublished master's thesis, Ball State University.

Auxter, D., Pyfer, J., & Huettig, C. (2005). *Principles and methods of adapted physical education and recreation.* McGraw-Hill: New York.

Block, M.E. (1995). Using peer tutors and task sheets. *Strategies, 8* (7), 9-14.

Block, M.E. (2007). *A teacher's guide to including students with disabilities in general physical education* (3rd ed.). Baltimore: Brookes.

Block, M.E., Oberweiser, B., & Bain, M. (1995). Utilizing classwide peer tutoring to facilitate inclusion of learners with disabilities in regular physical education. *Physical Educator, 52* (1), 47-56.

Bosworth, K. (1995). Caring for others and being cared for: Students talk caring in school. *Phi Delta Kappan, 76* (9), 686-693.

Briggs, D. (1975). Across the ages. *Times Educational Supplement, 15,* 9.

California Department of Education, Special Education Division. (2001). *Adapted physical education guidelines in California schools.* Sacramento, CA: Department of Education.

Centers for Disease Control and Prevention (CDC). (2004). *Physical activity and good nutrition: Essential elements to prevent chronic diseases and obesity.* Atlanta: National Center for Chronic Disease Prevention and Health Promotion.

Collier, D., & Hebert, F. (2004). Undergraduate physical education teacher preparation: What practitioners tell us. *Physical Educator, 61* (2), 102-112.

Daggett, S. (2004). Adapted physical education specialist, Liverpool Central School District, New York. Personal communication on training paraeducators in physical education.

Demchak, M. (1994). Helping individuals with severe disabilities find leisure activities. *Childhood Education, 69* (4), 234-236.

DePaepe, J.L. (1985). The influence of three least restrictive environments on the content, motor-ALT, and performance of moderately mentally retarded students. *Journal of Teaching in Physical Education, 3,* 34-41.

Dunlap, G., dePerczel, M., Clarke, S., Wilson, D., Wright, S., White, R., & Gomez, A. (1994). Choice making and proactive behavioral support for students with emotional and behavioral challenges. *Journal of Applied Behavior Analysis, 27,* 505-518.

Dunn, J.M., Morehouse, J.W., & Fredericks, H.D.B. (1986). *Physical education for the severely handicapped: A systematic approach to a data-based gymnasium.* Austin, TX: Pro-Ed.

Dyer, K., Dunlap, G., & Winterling, V. (1990). The effects of choice-making on the serious problem behaviors of students with severe handicaps. *Journal of Applied Behavior Analysis, 23,* 515-524.

Federal Register, March 12, 1999, PL 105-17, IDEA 1997.

Folsom-Meek, S.L. (1991). *Viewer's guide for Learning Together Series: Moving together.* Missouri TIKES federal grant, University of Missouri-Columbia.

Gable, R.A., Quinn, M.M., Rutherford, R.B., Howell, K.W., & Hoffman, C.C. (2000). Creating positive behavioral intervention plans and supports. Retrieved April 16, 2003, from http://cecp.air.org/fba/problembehavior3/main3.htm.

Garcia, R., & Krouscas, J.A. (1995). Build class community. *Strategies, 9* (2), 14-18.

Gartner, A., & Riessman, F. (1993). *Peer-tutoring: Towards a new model.* Washington, D.C.: ERIC Clearinghouse on Teaching and Teacher Education. (ERIC Document Reproduction Service No. ED36206)

Gaustad J. (1993). Peer and cross-age tutoring. *ERIC Digest, 7,* 1-7. Retrieved August 3, 2004, from http://eric.uoregon.edu/publication/digest/digest079.html.

Giangreco, M.F., Broer, S.M., & Edelman, S.W. (2002). "That was then, this is now!" Paraprofessional supports for students with disabilities in the general education classrooms. *Exceptionality, 10,* 47-64.

Giangreco, M.F., & Doyle, M.B. (2002). Students with disabilities and paraprofessional supports: Benefits, balance, and band aids. *Focus on Exceptional Children, 34* (7), 1-12.

Giangreco, M.F., Edelman, S.W., Luiselli, T.E., MacFarland, S.Z. (1997). Helping or hovering? Effects of instructional assistant proximity on students with disabilities. *Exceptional Children, 64* (1), 7-18.

Goodman, J., Sutton, V., & Harkavy, I. (1995). The effectiveness of family workshops in a middle school setting: Respect and caring make the difference. *Phi Delta Kappan, 76* (9), 694-700.

Graham, G., Holt-Hale, S.A., & Parker, M. (2007). *Children moving* (7th ed.). Boston: McGraw-Hill.

Himberg, C. (2004). Concerned Adults and Students for Physical Education Reform (CASPER). Retrieved August 8, 2004, from www.csuchico.edu/casper/quality_pe/index.html.

Himberg, C., Hutchinson, G.E., Roussell, J.M. (2003). *Teaching secondary physical education: Preparing adolescents to be active for life.* Champaign, IL: Human Kinetics.

Horner, R.H. (2000). Positive behavior supports. *Focus on Autism and Other Developmental Disabilities, 15* (2), 97-105.

Horton, M.L. (2001). Utilizing paraprofessionals in the general physical education setting. *Teaching Elementary Physical Education, 12* (6), 22-25.

Houston-Wilson, C., Lieberman, L.J., Horton, M., & Kasser, S. (1997). Peer tutoring: An effective strategy for inclusion. *Journal of Health, Physical Education, Recreation & Dance, 68* (6), 39-44.

Johnson, R.T., & Johnson, D.W. (1983). Effects of cooperative, competitive, and individualistic learning experiences on social development. *Exceptional Children, 49* (4), 323-329.

Karge, B., McClure, M., & Patton, P. (1995). The success of collaboration resource programs for students with disabilities in grades 6-8. *Remedial and Special Education, 16* (2), 79-89.

Karnes, M.B., & Esry, D.R. (1981). Working with parents of young exceptional children. *Educational Horizons, 59,* 143-149.

Kasser, S.L., & Lytle, R.K. (2005). *Inclusive physical activity: A lifetime of opportunities.* Champaign, IL: Human Kinetics.

Lavay, B.W., French, R., & Henderson, H.L. (2006). *Positive behavior management in physical activity settings* (2nd ed.). Champaign, IL: Human Kinetics.

Lieberman, L., & Houston-Wilson, C. (2002). *Strategies for inclusion: A handbook for physical educators.* Champaign, IL: Human Kinetics.

Lieberman, L.J., Newcomer, J., McCubbin, J., & Dalrymple, N. (1997). The effects of cross-aged peer tutors on the academic learning time of learners with disabilities in inclusive elementary physical education classes. *Brazilian International Journal of Adapted Physical Education Research, 4,* 15-32.

Long, E., Irmer, L., Burkett, L.N., Glasenapp, G., & Odenkirk, B. (1980). PEOPEL. *Journal of Physical Education, Recreation & Dance, 7* (51), 28-29.

Lytle, R., & Collier, D. (2002). The consultation process: Adapted physical education specialists' perceptions. *APAQ, 19* (3), 261-277.

Maurer, K. (2002). *The use of paraprofessionals in general physical education.* Unpublished master's thesis, SUNY Brockport.

Miller, L.J., & Cordova, J. (2002). Changing attitudes towards people with disabilities. *Palaestra, 18* (30), 16-21.

Modell, S., & Megginson, N. (2001). Life after school: A transition model for adapted physical educators. *Journal of Physical Education, Recreation and Dance, 72* (2), 45-48.

Mosston, M. (1966). *Teaching physical education.* Columbus, OH: Merrill.

National Association for Sport and Physical Education (NASPE). (2002). *Active start.* Reston, VA: NASPE.

National Association for Sport and Physical Education (NASPE). (2004). *Moving into the future* (2nd ed.). Reston, VA: McGraw-Hill.

National Consortium for Physical Education and Recreation for Individuals with Disabilities (NCPERID). (1995). *Adapted physical education national standards (APENS).* Champaign, IL: Human Kinetics.

Reams, D. (1997). Using teacher assistants in physical education classes serving students with disabilities. *Palaestra, 13* (2), 16-25.

Reddy, S.S., Utley, C.A., Delquadri, J.C., Mortweet, S.L., Greenwood, C.R., & Bowman, V. (1999). Peer tutoring for health and safety. *Teaching Exceptional Children, 31* (3) 45-52.

Reid, G., & O'Connor, J. (2003). The autism spectrum disorders: Activity selection, assessment, and program organization. *Palaestra, 19* (1), 20-27, 58.

Rink, J.E. (1998). *Teaching physical education for learning* (3rd ed.). Boston: McGraw-Hill.

Safran, S.P., & Oswald, K. (2003). Positive behavior supports: Can schools reshape disciplinary practices? *Exceptional Children, 69* (3), 361-373.

Schaps, E., & Lewis, C. (1998). Breeding citizenship through community in school. *Education Digest, 64,* 23-27.

Schultheis, S.F., Boswell, B.B., & Decker, J. (2000). Successful physical activity programming for students with autism. *Focus on Autism and Other Developmental Disabilities, 15,* 159-162.

Seaman, J.A., DePauw, K.P., Morton, K.B., & Omoto, K. (2003). *Making connections: From theory to practice in adapted physical education.* Scottsdale, AZ: Holcomb Hathaway.

Siedentop, D., & Tannehill, D. (2000). *Developing teaching skills in physical education* (4th ed.). Mountain View, CA: Mayfield.

Sherrill, C. (1993). *Adapted physical activity, recreation and sport: Crossdisciplinary and lifespan* (4th ed.). Madison, WI: Brown.

Sherrill, C. (2004). *Adapted physical activity, recreation, and sport: Crossdisciplinary and lifespan.* Boston: McGraw-Hill.

Short, F.X. (2005). Measurement, assessment, and program evaluation. In J.P. Winnick (Ed.), *Adapted physical education and sport* (4th ed.) (pp. 55-75). Champaign, IL: Human Kinetics.

Sinibaldi, R. (2001). Peers: Partnerships for equals, exceptional and regular students. *Strategies, 14* (4), 9-13.

Special Olympics. (1989). *Motor activities training program*. Washington, D.C.: Author.

Stainback, S., & Stainback, W. (1990). Inclusive schooling. In W. Stainback & S. Stainback (Eds.), *Supporting networks for inclusive schooling* (pp. 3-24). Baltimore: Brookes.

Stainback, S., & Stainback, W. (1996). *Inclusion: A guide for educators*. Baltimore: Brookes.

Sugai, G., & Horner, R. (2001). *School climate and discipline: Going to scale*. Paper presented at the national summit on the shared implementation of IDEA. Retrieved April 20, 2003, from www.pbis.org.

Turnbull, A., Edmondson, H., Griggs, P., Wickham, D., Sailor, W., Freeman, R., Guess, D., Lasson, S., McCart, A., Park, J., Riffel, L., Turnbull, R., & Warren, J. (2002). A blueprint for schoolwide positive behavior support: Implementation of three components. *Exceptional Children, 3* (68), 377-402.

U.S. Department of Health and Human Services. (1996). *Physical activity and health: A report of the surgeon general*. Atlanta, GA: U.S. Department of Health and Human Services, Centers for Disease Control and Prevention, National Center for Chronic Disease Prevention and Health Promotion.

U.S. Department of Health and Human Services. (2004). *Healthy People 2010*. Washington, DC: Author.

Webster, G.E. (1987). Influence of peer tutors on academic learning time—physical education of mentally handicapped students. *Journal of Teaching in Physical Education, 6*, 393-403.

Wentzel, K.R. (1997). Student motivation in middle school: The role of perceived pedagogical caring. *Journal of Educational Psychology, 89*, 41-49.

Winnick, J.P. (Ed.). (2000). *Adapted physical education and sport* (3rd ed.). Champaign, IL: Human Kinetics.

Wolery, M., Bailey, D.B., & Sugai, G.M. (1988). *Effective teaching: Principles of applied behavior analysis with exceptional students*. Boston: Allyn & Bacon.

Additional Resources

Cox, L., & Lubbers, T. (1999). *Make it, take it: Creating movement challenge kits for play at home or school*. Kearney, NE: Tekna Books. Can be obtained for $19.95 plus $3.00 shipping and handling from Lynn Cox, 6200 Cardinal Road, Excelsior, MN 55331 or Terry Lubbers, 10456 Cavell Avenue South, Bloomington, MN 55438.

Doyle, M.B. (1997). *The paraprofessional's guide to the inclusive classroom*. Baltimore: Brookes.

FlagHouse
601 FlagHouse Dr.
Hasbrouck Heights, NJ 07604-3116
Telephone: 800-793-7900
Fax: 800-793-7922
www.flaghouse.com

Gopher Sport
P.O. Box 998
Owatonna, MN 55060
Telephone: 800-533-0445
Fax: 800-451-4855
www.gophersport.com

Human Kinetics
P.O. Box 5076
Champaign, IL 61825-5076
800-747-4457
www.HumanKinetics.com

Kasser, S.L. (1995). *Games: Movement fun for everyone*. Champaign, IL: Human Kinetics.

Lieberman, L., & Cowart, J. (1996). *Games for people with sensory impairments: Strategies for including individuals of all ages*. Champaign, IL: Human Kinetics.

Lieberman, L., & Houston-Wilson, C. (2002). *Strategies for inclusion: A handbook for physical educators*. Champaign, IL: Human Kinetics.

Morris, L.R., & Schulz, L. (1989). *Creative play activities for children with disabilities: A resource book for children and parents*. Champaign, IL: Human Kinetics.

Pacer (Parent Advocacy Coalition for Educational Rights): www.pacer.org

PE Central. (n.d.). Adaptations for physical activities. Retrieved June 18, 2004, from www.pecentral.org/adapted/adaptedactivities.html.

Special Olympics
1133 19th St. NW
Washington, D.C. 20036
202-628-3630
www.specialolympics.org

Special Olympics. (1989). *Motor activities training program*. Washington, D.C.: Author.

Sports 'N Spokes
Paralyzed Veterans of America
801 18th St. NW
Washington, D.C. 20006-3517
888-888-2201
www.pvamagazine.com/sns

United States Government. (n.d.). *IDEA 1997 final regulations*. Retrieved July 26, 2004, from www.ideapractices.org/law/regulations/topicIndex.php.

Videos

Insight Media
2162 Broadway
New York, NY 10024-0621
800-233-9910

- IEPs: Avoiding Planning Pitfalls, #TAE2628, 14 minutes, $139
- IEPs: Critical Content Components, #TAE2629, 18 minutes, $139

Web Sites

Information about IEPs and the IEP process:

- www.ed.gov/parents/needs/speced/iepguide/index.html
- www.angelfire.com/ny/Debsimms/education.html

Information about ITPs:

- www.schwablearning.org/articles.aspx?r=998&f=relatedlink

About the Contributors

Rocco Aiello

Rocco Aiello is a nationally certified adapted physical education instructor (CAPE) working for the St. Mary's County Public Schools. Rocco teaches students with disabilities at the high school level and is a consultant for all physical education teachers in the St. Mary's County Public Schools. Rocco is the section chair for adapted physical education for the Maryland Association of Health, Physical Education, Recreation and Dance (MAHPERD) and is the chairperson for the Maryland Consortium of Adapted Physical Education. Rocco is a graduate from SUNY Brockport, in Brockport, New York, and holds a master's degree in adapted physical education with an emphasis in early childhood. He also obtained a post-master's degree in administration and supervision from Towson University, Towson, Maryland.

Dr. Douglas Collier

Douglas Collier received his bachelor's and master's degrees, as well as a diploma in special education, from McGill University and his doctorate from Indiana University. Doug works in the adapted physical education graduate program as well as teaching undergraduate courses in the teacher preparation program with an emphasis on elementary and early childhood education. In addition, he is the coordinator of the undergraduate physical education teacher certification program at SUNY Brockport. His research, writing, and presentations focus on positive educative approaches to behavior management, the autism spectrum disorder, as well as effectively teaching students in urban educational settings. Doug joined the SUNY Brockport faculty in 2003 and has taught in higher education since 1993. Doug has taught adapted physical education in a variety of settings since 1976.

Dr. Ronald W. Davis

Dr. Davis was a professor of adapted physical education at Ball State University and now teaches adapted physical education at Texas Woman's University. He received his PhD from Texas Woman's University and his master's degree from the University of Wisconsin-LaCrosse. He is the author of the book *Inclusion Through Sports* (Human Kinetics, 2002).

Dr. Sherry L. Folsom-Meek

Sherry Folsom-Meek, PhD, is professor and coordinator of the Developmental Adapted Physical Education (DAPE) Teacher Licensure Program at Minnesota State University, Mankato. She teaches courses in DAPE and research methods (graduate). Sherry's primary research interests are attitudes of preservice physical education teachers toward teaching learners with disabilities and transition. She is a past president of MnAHPERD and was the Central District AAHPERD Scholar in 2002. Her greatest joy is seeing her students make a difference in the lives of people with disabilities.

Jayne McBride Glidewell, MA, CAPE

Jayne has been a specialist in physical education and adapted physical education for 28 years. Currently, she works for the Nevada Joint Union High School District as a district adapted physical education specialist and peer-tutor coordinator for special education. Past recognitions include Teacher of the Year, Teacher Who Makes a Difference, and Wells Fargo Teacher of the Year. Most recent areas of special interest are inclusion, peer tutor programs and training, and the ongoing development of the critical role of paraeducators in physical education.

Ileah Jackson

Ileah Jackson is an adapted physical education teacher for San Juan Unified School District in Sacramento, California. She is currently working on her master's degree in special education at California State University in Sacramento. Ms. Jackson has presented at numerous national conferences on adapted physical activity. She is active in the community directing programs for individuals with disabilities and holding play-based workshops. In 2004, Ms. Jackson received the Julius Spizzirri Student Scholarship for exemplary student teaching in the field of adapted physical education. She was recently inducted into the Shasta College Athletic Hall of Fame.

Dr. Ellen Kowalski

Ellen M. Kowalski, PhD, is an associate professor in the Department of Health Studies, Physical Education, and Human Performance Science at Adelphi University. She teaches in the areas of adapted physical education, motor development, motor learning, and rhythms and movement fundamentals in the teacher preparation curriculum.

Dr. Lauren J. Lieberman

Lauren graduated with a PhD from Oregon State University in human performance with an emphasis in movement studies in disabilities and a minor in special education. She received her master's degree from the University of Wisconsin-LaCrosse in special physical education and her bachelor's degree from West Chester University in health and physical education with a concentration in adapted physical education. Prior to graduate school, she taught at the Perkins School for the Blind in the deafblind program for 5 years. She taught physical education and swimming, and she coached track and field, goalball, and swimming. Lauren is currently a professor at SUNY Brockport in the area of adapted physical education. She is also the undergraduate coordinator of the adapted physical education concentration. She has been teaching at SUNY Brockport since 1995. She supervises practicum experiences at both the undergraduate and graduate level. She also runs Camp Abilities, a developmental summer sport camp for children with visual impairments. Her areas of research include inclusion strategies and physical activity for youths with sensory impairments. She has written several books, including *Games for People With Sensory Impairments,* cowritten with Jim Cowart; *Strategies for Inclusion,* cowritten with Dr. Cathy Houston-Wilson; and *Case Studies in Adapted Physical Education,* with three coauthors. *Transition Guidelines for Community-Based Physical Activities for Students Who Have Visual Impairments, Blindness, or Deafblindness* was published through the American Printing House for the Blind. She is currently chair of the AAHPERD Adapted Physical Activity Council.

Dr. Rebecca Lytle

Dr. Rebecca Lytle is an associate professor at California State University, Chico (CSU). She taught adapted physical education in the public schools for 10 years before becoming a faculty member at CSU. As an adapted physical education specialist, she worked with paraeducators daily and values the important work that they do for children. Currently she is the coordinator of the Adapted Physical Education Credential Program at CSU and oversees three clinics for individuals with disabilities. She has presented and published at the state, national, and international levels. Her research areas of interest include parent perceptions, autism, consultation, and teacher training.

Dr. Scott Modell

Dr. Modell is a professor at California State University, Sacramento. He has taught adapted physical education in public schools both at the elementary and secondary level. He has presented numerous papers regionally, nationally, and internationally on the provision of adapted physical education services for students with disabilities. He has also developed a number of community-based sport programs for youths and adults with disabilities. For his work in this area, he has received the Distinguished Faculty Award for Service, Outstanding Community Service Award, and Exemplary Program for Adapted Physical Education.

Carin Mulawka

Carin Mulawka is a physical education and adapted physical education teacher in Rochester, New York. Carin has many years of experience working with students who have a wide range of disabilities in a physical education setting as well as working with paraprofessionals. She attended SUNY Brockport for her bachelor's degree and the University of Wisconsin-La Crosse for her master's degree.

Amy Oliver

Amy Oliver is a physical educator at Southside High School in Muncie Community Schools. She received her master's degree in adapted physical education from Ball State University. She studied paraeducators while conducting research for her thesis.

Dr. Cindy K. Piletic

Dr. Cindy Piletic is an associate professor of adapted physical education at Western Illinois University. She received her PhD from Texas Woman's University and her master's degree from Western Illinois University.

Dr. Carol Ryan

Carol earned her bachelor's and master's degrees in health and physical education from the University of North Carolina, and she earned a doctorate from the University of Cincinnati with an emphasis in motor development and behavior. Carol taught elementary physical education for 6 years and adapted physical education for 6 years, and she has been a professor of physical education at Northern Kentucky University since 1996. Carol is currently serving as the associate dean of the College of Education and Human Services at Northern Kentucky University.

About the Editor

Lauren J. Lieberman earned her PhD at Oregon State University in human performance, with an emphasis in movement studies in disabilities and a minor in special education. She received her MS from the University of Wisconsin at LaCrosse in special physical education. She earned her BS from West Chester University, in Pennsylvania, in health and physical education with a concentration in adapted physical education. Prior to graduate school she taught in the deafblind program at the Perkins School for the Blind in Watertown, Massachusetts, for 5 years. There she worked with many paraeducators and learned the true value of having them on her team.

Lauren is currently a full professor at the State University of New York (SUNY) at Brockport in adapted physical education, and she is the undergraduate coordinator of adapted physical education. She has been teaching at SUNY Brockport since 1995. Lauren teaches graduate and undergraduate classes in adapted physical education and supervises practicum experiences at both the undergraduate and graduate level. Each summer, she runs Camp Abilities, a developmental sports camp for children with visual impairments. Her areas of research are inclusion strategies and physical activity for youth with sensory impairments. She has written four books: *Games for People With Sensory Impairments* (cowritten with Jim Cowart); *Strategies for Inclusion* (cowritten with Dr. Cathy Houston-Wilson), and *Case Studies in Adapted Physical Education* (with three coauthors). She is coauthor of the book *Going Places: A Transition Guide to Physical Activity for Youth With Visual Impairments or Deafblindness,* which was published in 2006 through the American Printing House for the Blind. Lauren is currently the chair of the Adapted Physical Activity Council, which is the national Adapted Physical Education organization through the American Alliance for Health, Physical Education, Recreation and Dance.

You'll find other outstanding adapted physical education resources at

www.HumanKinetics.com

In the U.S. call

1-800-747-4457

Australia...08 8372 0999
Canada 1-800-465-7301
Europe..+44 (0) 113 255 5665
New Zealand.......................................0064 9 448 1207

HUMAN KINETICS
The Information Leader in Physical Activity
P.O. Box 5076 • Champaign, IL 61825-5076 USA